The Bristol Rovers Archive

NUMBER 1

1951-1991

Keith Brookman, who lives in Bristol, has been the
editor of the Bristol Rovers matchday magazine,
'The Pirate', since 1996.

Alan Marshall, who now lives in Spain,
was the Bristol Rovers Official Club Photographer
for thirty years, from 1974.

Both are lifelong Bristol Rovers supporters and look forward to collaborating
on further volumes of photographs of the club.

First published 2012 by
Tangent Books
Unit 5.16 Paintworks
Arnos Vale
Bristol
BS4 3EH

0117 972 0645

www.tangentbooks.co.uk

Publisher: Richard Jones Richard@tangentbooks.co.uk

ISBN 978-1906477-75-2

Design: Ann Walter
Cover Design: Joe Burt, Ann Walter
Production: Chris Swift

A CIP record for this book is available from the British Library

Printed in the UK using paper from a sustainable source.

Preface

In season 1952/53 Bristol Rovers won their first ever Football League promotion, capturing the Third Division (South) title. While this book is not a diamond anniversary tribute to that team, it was the spur needed to produce this book, which brings together a collection of photos spanning forty years in the proud history of the club.

The first images are from 1951 when Rovers reached the quarter-final of the FA Cup, going out to the eventual winners of the competition, Newcastle United, after a replay that caught the imagination of the Bristol footballing public.

The selected photos from the 1950s, widely regarded as a golden age for Bristol Rovers, feature many of the players and staff who, even today, retain a place in the history of this great club. Perhaps that's because they played alongside each other for so many years; the team of the 1950s virtually picked itself.

The club's 'No Buy, No Sell' policy also contributed to the camaraderie of that side and their closeness to the supporters and, hopefully, the small selection of photographs from that time illustrates that point.

Appropriately the first image is of influential skipper Ray Warren, a player whose career began before the Second World War, pictured at a flooded Eastville. We then move on to take in a number of the players who represented this proud club during those halcyon days.

Harry Bamford, Alfie Biggs Geoff Bradford, Geoff Fox, Bert Hoyle, Barrie Meyer, George Petherbridge, Jack Pitt, and Dai Ward, not forgetting manager Bert Tann, are among those featured from a time when football was a totally different game from the one we know today.

As well as the floods at Eastville, we see camping under canvas at Weston and training at Southend prior to a cup tie at Newcastle (though why they didn't set up a training camp in the north east is a little bit of a mystery, at least to me). Perhaps the most treasured photo among them, though, is the one featuring the heading practice with trainer Bert Williams – imagine that scene today!

From the success of the 1950s we move on to the dawn of a new decade and whilst it is known affectionately as the Swinging Sixties, for Rovers it was anything but. Relegated to the Third Division in 1963, the famous quartered shirts were ditched in favour of blue and white stripes and then an all blue strip. There were, also, new names on the teamsheet for the next generation of supporters to remember. Bernard Hall, Ian Hamilton, Doug Hillard, Harold Jarman, and Bobby Jones are just a few of the new heroes to emerge, while the evergreen Alfie Biggs resumed his Rovers career following a brief interlude at Deepdale with Preston North End.

Still ensconced in the Third Division as we entered the1970s, Rovers enjoyed two seasons of success in the Football League Cup, reaching the fifth round in 1970/71 and again in 1971/72. The appointment of Don Megson as manager heralded a new period of success. The Watney Cup was won in 1972 and promotion back to the second tier of English football achieved in 1974.

The promotion success came about because Megson had built a wonderfully consistent team that worked so hard for each other and included the goalscoring talents of Alan Warboys and Bruce Bannister, alias 'Smash and Grab'. As well as Warboys and Bannister, another raft of players emerged before, during and after the promotion success, Colin Dobson, Mike Green, Lindsay Parsons, Frankie Prince, Dick Sheppard, Kenny Stephens and Stuart Taylor among them.

Eastville, the proud home of Bristol's oldest professional football club, played host to many marvellous games during this decade, but it was all about to change as we entered the 1980s. Bobby Campbell had succeeded Megson as manager, before Harold Jarman took over in a temporary capacity. He was replaced by Terry Cooper and the former England international defender was in charge of the club at the time of the Eastville fire in 1980.

A handful of games were played at Ashton Gate while Eastville was being prepared to host football once again. However, playing in what resembled a shell of the former stadium following the fire just wasn't the same and a disastrous season ended in relegation to the Third Division.

Bobby Gould came and went as manager on two occasions and, amazingly, England World Cup winner Alan Ball ended his playing career with Bristol Rovers. The club celebrated its centenary with games against Tottenham Hotspur, Newcastle United and Wotton, and a number of players emerged who were to go on to enjoy careers at the highest level. Among them were Ian Holloway, Phil Kite, Gary Mabbutt, Tony Pulis, David Williams and Geraint Williams. We shouldn't forget Micky Barrett, either, who would surely have gone on to enjoy a successful career had he not been struck down with cancer, passing away at the age of 24.

The 1980s saw Rovers leave Eastville for the last time, beginning a decade in exile in Bath, playing home games at Bath City's tiny Twerton Park ground. Amazingly, under the astute guidance of former England international, Gerry Francis fortunes changed yet again and in 1990 he led the side to the Third Division title and to a first ever appearance at Wembley.

Ian Alexander, Vaughan Jones, David Mehew, Brian Parkin, Andy Reece, Carl Saunders, Geoff Twentyman and Devon White were the latest in a long line of crowd favourites. Our journey from the past ends forty years after the first photo in this book, with Rovers still playing at Twerton Park.

It is hoped that this book is the first in a series of photographic images to complement the historical reference books of the club that have already been published.

Keith Brookman

With grateful thanks to the following

Former Rovers club photographer Alan Marshall who took, or copied, the majority of the images I hope you have enjoyed looking at again, or for the first time.

To Ray Warren's daughter, Anita Mason, who allowed Alan to copy the photographs of her father's Rovers career.

To Harold Jarman, who lent me a collection of photos from his time at the club, many of which were taken by Alan. A number of those photos are included here and there are others that will, hopefully, be included in a second volume.

To Bobby Jones for the photos used from his collection.

To club historian Mike Jay who shared some of his collection of Alan Marshall's Rovers photos with me and, through his historical reference books on the club on his own or in collaboration with others, inspired me to go into print myself!

To Sean Ryan, who gave me a number of the photos used in this publication. Sean began supporting Rovers in the late 1950s and used to travel over from Ireland, as a young man, in the early 1960s. He still travels over two or three times every season.

To the Bamford family, who also lent me some of the photos of Harry Bamford in thier possession.

To Paul Mills, of Pensord, and Richard Jones of Tangent Books for their support in getting this project up and running.

Last, but by no means least, thanks to designer Ann Walter without whom it would not have been possible to bring you this collection of historic club photos, reproduced in one volume for the first time.

Photo Index
(Listed by Player)

This photo was taken at Eastville in January 1951, just days before Rovers were due to host Aldershot in the third round of the FA Cup.

Skipper Ray Warren is seen surveying the flooded pitch which was under three feet of water and he must have been thinking it would have been more appropriate to have a fishing rod in his hands, rather than a football under his arm!

Amazingly the cup tie went ahead once the waters had subsided and, on 10th January 1951, Rovers registered a comfortable 5-1 win against their opponents when a crowd of 13,249 saw Vic Lambden score a hat-trick, with Bill Roost and George Petherbridge adding further goals.

The team that day was: Hoyle, Bamford, Fox, Pitt, Warren, Sampson, Petherbridge, Bradford, Lambden, Roost, Watling.

It was Rovers' seventh cup tie of the season, as they had taken three games to overcome Llanelli in the first round, and another three to edge past Gillingham in round two.

In the fourth round they beat Luton 2-1 at Kenilworth Road, and a Hull City side which included the legendary Raich Carter and future England manager Don Revie went down 3-0 at Eastville in the fifth round.

Rovers were drawn away to Newcastle in the quarter-finals of the competition. A 0-0 draw with the First Division outfit at St James' Park was followed by a 3-1 defeat at Eastville just four days later, a game that saw queues of up to 100,000 wanting tickets.

Newcastle went on to win the FA Cup, and the same eleven players who had faced Rovers in both games between the clubs beat Blackpool 2-0 at Wembley.

Rovers have since reached the quarter-finals of the competition on two more occasions. In 1957/58 they lost 3-1 to Fulham at Craven Cottage after entering at the Third Round stage, and beating Mansfield, Burnley (after a replay) and Bristol City before facing the Cottagers.

In 2007/08, Rovers came in at the first round stage and beat Leyton Orient (after a replay), Rushden & Diamonds, Fulham (after a replay), Barnet and Southampton before losing to West Bromwich Albion at the Memorial Stadium.

Ray Warren, born in Bristol in 1918, had signed for Rovers as an amateur in 1934. After signing pro forms in 1936, he made his debut in March of that year.

Resuming his career after the Second World War, he went on to skipper the side to promotion in 1953 and by the time of his retirement in 1956, he had made a total of 450 league appearances for the club.

It Might Take A Stud!

No Expense Spared

It appears that no expense was spared, in terms of preparing for the aforementioned FA Cup quarter-final tie at St James' Park on 24th February 1951.

For some reason, training for the biggest game in the club's history took place at Southend, where this photo was taken on the Tuesday prior to the game.

Manager Bert Tann holds a tray of oysters and the players all get stuck in to the sea food, reputed to be 'tasty and stamina building' though they have been known for other things as well!

From left to right, the players are Bryan Bush, Bert Hoyle, Jack Pitt, Harry Bamford, George Petherbridge, Ray Warren and Geoff Bradford who is next to trainer Bert Williams. I'm pretty certain that the player between Hoyle and Pitt is Vic Lambden and that it's Bill Roost between Bradford and Williams.

Evening World reporter Pat Kavanagh, who covered the training sessions at Southend, had this to say about the preparations. 'As Rovers manager Bert Tann added the final touches to their training, the style the Bristol lads will use against Newcastle became plain.

'The defence had to run up to an imaginary line, stop abruptly, turn, and then sprint at maximum speed in the direction from which they had come.

'Speed was the keynote – speed in covering up, should a defender be beaten in a tackle; speed in returning to the tackle a second and third time if necessary.

'The forwards practised short sprints from a standing start; sharp bursts of speed after a quick turn.

'Speed again – speed which it is hoped will send the Bristol forwards racing through a Newcastle defence which does not move too quickly.'

Training at Southend came to an end two days before the game and, on the Thursday evening, the players attended a show in Southend before setting off for Whitley Bay on the Friday.

Kavanagh concluded his report by saying: 'So twelve Rovers players are waiting for the big day, fit as fiddles, determined and convinced that they can shake this much vaunted Newcastle team right out of the Cup.'

They almost did it, of course, and drew 0-0. The replay took place at Eastville on the following Wednesday, and although Geoff Bradford gave Rovers an early lead in that match, the visitors hit back to win 3-1 and went on to win the Cup.

Over 60,000 watched the first encounter and more than 30,000 were at Eastville to witness the replay.

The gentleman stood on the step ladder dangling a football on what resembles a fishing rod is Bert Williams, who was the club's senior trainer from 1945 to 1962.

This photo was taken the day before the FA Cup replay against Newcastle, at Eastville in 1951. The players practicing their heading skills are Geoff Fox, Ray Warren and Jackie Pitt, who were all first team regulars from the late 1940s to the mid 1950s.

Defender Fox was born in Bristol and signed amateur forms for Ipswich in 1942, becoming a full time professional with them in 1945 after a brief stint as an amateur with Bristol City. After 12 games for the East Anglian side he signed for Rovers in 1947 and went on to appear in 274 league games for the club.

Warren played for Rovers either side of the Second World War. An ever-present for five seasons, he was awarded benefit matches in 1946 and 1947 and skippered the side which won the Third Division (South) title in 1952/53. In all, he appeared in 450 league games whilst at Eastville.

Pitt was 26 before he made his league debut for Rovers, but went on to play in 467 league games before his retirement. His association with the club continued long after he hung up his boots. Initially he coached the club's youngsters and then became groundsman, firstly at Eastville, and then at Twerton Park.

Williams joined the club as groundsman in 1920, and was appointed assistant trainer in 1923, a post he held until the outbreak of the Second World War. He stepped up to the role of senior trainer in 1945 and was awarded a testimonial match

in 1962 when Sheffield Wednesday provided the opposition on 30th October.

The programme for that match had this to say about him.

'Between the Wars young players who passed through his hands to make their names in the game included Cliff Britton, Joe Calvert, Ronnie Dix, Steve Sims, David Steele, Phil Taylor and Joe Walter. He has, of course, been responsible for the fitness of all the outstanding Rovers players who have served the club so well since 1945. Bert Williams will be remembered by many local amateur clubs and players, both soccer and rugger, for the help they received from him.'

Presumably his training methods, which seem a little bit eccentric some sixty years later, worked as the successful Rovers team of the 1950s went so close to gaining promotion to the First Division.

Don't expect them to be re-introduced, though, as the health and safety police would have a field day if they caught any of our current coaches standing on a step ladder without a safety net!

Heading Practice

Harry in Australia

In 1951, Rovers full-back Harry Bamford was selected for the FA touring Party to Australia and is seen here at the front of the group getting off their plane at Perth.

The tourists, whilst not considered strong enough to be regarded as an England 'B' team, were still strong enough to win all 20 of the games played on the 11-week tour, scoring 153 goals and conceding just 14.

The full party for the tour was as follows: Langton (Bolton), Broome (Notts County), Burgin (Sheffield United), Webster (Bolton), Clarke (Portsmouth), Parker (West Ham), Kieran (Tranmere), Smith (Birmingham), Bartram (Charlton), Bamford (Bristol Rovers), McCue (Stoke), Shaw (Sheffield United), Hurst (Charlton), Sewell (Sheffield United), Flewin (Portsmouth), Owen (Luton), Lock (Charlton), Hagan (Sheffield United).

The five 'Test' matches against the host nation were won by scores of 4-1, 17-0, 4-1, 6-1 and 5-0 and Bamford certainly made an impression every time he played.

This is what one Australian reporter wrote midway through the tour: *'Despite the galaxy of stars in the England side, the man that appeals most to Australian football fans is big Bristol Rovers full-back Harry Bamford.*

'He has played in every match of the tour so far. Possessing the pace of a forward, Bamford has been a stumbling block to the Australian players he has met so far.'

Although he had been playing at right back for much of his career, Bamford had been a centre-forward as a schoolboy and he was selected in that position for the tourists' game against Granville District and scored twice in a 5-2 win.

Bamford had joined Rovers in 1945 and went on to make 486 league appearances in the famous blue and white quarters. He was an ever-present in the promotion-winning team of 1952/53 and was a defender who preferred to play his way out of trouble rather than boot it into the stand.

A keep fit fanatic, he was also a keen pigeon racer and whilst in Australia, his birds won the first three prizes in the Bristol St Philip's Flying Club's race from Barnt Green and the news of his success was cabled to him.

Sadly, Bamford was involved in a road accident in October 1958 when his motor cycle was involved in a collision with a car as he was returning home after coaching at Clifton College and he died in hospital on 31st October.

The Harry Bamford Memorial Trophy, in his memory, was awarded each year to a deserving local sportsman.

This photo was taken at the FA Cup tie between Rovers and Huddersfield at Leeds Road on 10th January 1953.

As the Evening World caption tells us, home goalkeeper Wheeler punches clear as Rovers centre-forward Vic Lambden jumps to meet a centre, with Paddy Leonard (8) and Geoff Bradford waiting for a possible mistake or rebound.

As it was an Evening World photo, it was to that newspaper I turned for the match facts of a game that Rovers lost 2-0.

Reporter Pat Kavanagh said: 'Rovers battling against odds all the way, were beaten 2-0 at Huddersfield in the Cup today.

'It was their first defeat in 22 games. They gave a gallant display and were not dismayed when, a goal down, they lost goalkeeper Hoyle. Lambden went in goal until Hoyle returned with his head bandaged.'

Playing on what was described as a wide pitch, it appears that Rovers took a while to adapt, but when they did Watling forced a save from Wheeler and then Rovers had three chances in quick succession but shots from Lambden, Watling and Leonard were all cleared off the line.

Hoyle saved well from Metcalfe, but just as it seemed as though the first half would end goalless, the home side took the lead two minutes before the break: 'I thought the Rovers were a shade fortunate when the referee awarded a free kick instead of a penalty when Warren brought down Glazzard, but it brought a goal anyway.

'Metcalfe's free kick found Glazzard in an unmarked position and the centre-forward headed in, well out of Hoyle's reach.'

Hoyle was injured in the second half, when he dived at Glazzard's feet and had to leave the pitch for treatment.

'The incident was a tragedy for Rovers and after Hoyle was led to the dressing room Lambden took his place with Bradford moving to centre-forward.

'Lambden earned applause for a save he made from Metcalfe, but conceded a goal when Watson headed home a centre from Metcalfe.'

It was one of the few games that Paddy Leonard played for the club during his two seasons at Eastville, and the only FA Cup tie he appeared in.

A crowd of 34,967, which included 4,000 Rovers fans, were at Leeds Road and saw the following Rovers side in action: Hoyle, Bamford, Fox, Pitt, Warren, Sampson, Bush, Leonard, Lambden, Bradford, Watling.

Two days after their cup defeat, Rovers travelled for a week's stay at Bognor Regis, a trip described as part holiday, part 'toning up' to prepare for the strenuous league programme ahead.

Unbeaten Run Comes To An End

A First For Bradford

Taken at Eastville, on 3rd October 1953, when Rovers beat Hull City 4-2, this photo shows Geoff Bradford putting Rovers 3-2 ahead.

It was the club's first season in the Second Division and they had made a solid start, winning four, losing four and drawing three of the 11 games played before this one.

Rovers ran out comfortable winners on this occasion, with Bill Roost (2), 'Josser' Watling and Bradford on the scoresheet.

The report of the match began with fulsome praise for Bradford: *'Bristol Rovers did very well indeed to beat Hull City, in what was a real thriller. They were twice in arrears and did not take the lead until the 52nd minute when Geoff Bradford netted his first goal at Eastville since that great hat-trick on 25th April, against Newport County, which made promotion safe.*

'Bradford was the most outstanding forward on the field. He was opposed by former England centre-half Neil Franklin, but that did not worry him in the least.'

The visitors had taken the lead after 18 minutes, against the run of play, when goalkeeper Howard Radford misjudged a lobbed ball into the goalmouth by Ken Harrison. It took just eight minutes for the equaliser to arrive, when Bryan Bush found an unmarked Watling and his low shot beat goalkeeper Tom Forgan.

Hull regained the lead on 35 minutes, when Hans Jensen's free kick was placed just wide of the defensive wall, giving John Tarrant the chance to lob the ball over Radford.

A second equaliser arrived before half time, when George Petherbridge headed a clearance back across goal to Roost, who hooked the ball in from close range.

Bradford then gave Rovers the lead shortly after half time: *'A move initiated by Sampson, and carried on by Watling, gave Rovers the lead for the first time. As Roost centred, Bradford raced in and took the ball away from Forgan's hands, brought it under control, and flicked it into an empty net.'*

There were 68 minutes on the clock when the fourth goal was scored. Bradford's shot hit Franklin and rebounded to Roost, who steadied himself before firing a shot past Forgan.

In front of an Eastville crowd of 25,224, Rovers lined up as follows: Radford, Bamford, Fox, Pitt, Warren, Sampson, Petherbridge, Roost, Bradford, Bush, Watling.

It proved to be a very satisfying inaugural season at the higher level for Rovers, as they finished in ninth place, with 44 points.

Hull managed six points fewer and ended the campaign in fifteenth place, while Leicester City were Second Division champions, and Everton claimed the runners-up spot.

This photo shows Norman Sykes shaking hands with Geoff Bradford, watched by manager Bert Tann, and was taken on the day the young defender signed his first pro contract for the club.

The photo appeared in the local press that same day, 15th October 1953.

Born in Bristol, Sykes captained Bristol Boys and represented England Schoolboys in 1951/52. In 1953 he played for the England Youth side.

*In his book, Edward Giles tells the story of how he became a Rovers player:

'Rovers had to resort to subterfuge to sign him as a professional after he had played in their reserve side at the age of 16.

'Word having got round that other clubs were interested in him, Rovers turned to Bert Hoyle for assistance, and their former goalkeeper took Sykes away to stay with relatives of Hoyle's in Bradford for a week.

'The day before his 17th birthday in October 1953, Sykes travelled with Hoyle to London, to join up with Bert Tann and Geoff Bradford, who were there for the match in which Bradford scored three of an FA team's four goals in the defeat of an RAF side at Tottenham.

'On the train back from Paddington to Temple Meads in Bristol, the four men checked their watches and, one minute before midnight, Tann produced the forms that Sykes signed to become a Rovers professional and collect the £10 signing-on fee, which was all that could be legally allowed.'

His Rovers career wasn't without moments of controversy.

Following his debut, against Bury on Boxing Day 1956, he went on to become the club's youngest captain when, aged 22, he skippered the side against Fulham in January 1959.

A year later he asked for a transfer, then withdrew his request before asking for a move again. There were no takers when he was placed on the transfer list with a £25,000 fee on his head and he took part in a fruitless trial with Chelsea before he signed another contract at Eastville.

Troubled by a persistent knee injury towards the end of his time with the club, he decided to retire from the game, though he was tempted to return to football in Canada, and played for Toronto City before linking up with Plymouth Argyle, for whom he played just three games.

He later made 52 league appearances for Stockport and a further 15 for Doncaster Rovers, before playing non-league football for Altrincham and opening a teetotal night club in Manchester.

* Bristol Rovers, The Bert Tann Era, by Edward Giles, published by Desert Island Books

Sykes On Board

Under Canvas

As part of pre season preparations for the 1954/55 season, Rovers manager Bert Tann took his players to Weston for a fortnight, where they used the Weston St John's ground and slept under canvas.

The practice was definitely repeated over the next two years and, I believe, continued for longer than that. My guess is that this photo was taken in the summer of 1954. It shows Ray Warren and Jack Pitt handing out the mattresses for their team-mates, who made sure that they were taken into the marquee, just about visible to the left of the photo.

One local journalist spent some time with the club at that first camp, and filed this report: *'Bristol Rovers open air training camp at Weston super Mare is a great success. It is not a stunt and I am convinced that other football clubs will soon start searching for similar sites.*

'At first I wasn't impressed with tales that this type of training had made World Champions of Germany and Uruguay. That's why I visited the Rovers, ate in their Nissen hut and took part in every activity – just like a player.

'Completely converted, I was sorry to leave the camp. Rovers' manager Bert Tann also had his doubts and told me that he didn't claim that better playing results would follow, but that it was something new and worth trying.

'Reveille (BBC pips on a battery portable) starts the day, at 7.00am. *The keen types hop out of bed, run 200 yards across Weston golf course and have a dip in the sea.*

'Breakfast is at 8.30am, with men on the duty roster serving. Everyone, including the manager is on the roster. Intensive ball practice, with hundreds of holidaymakers watching, fills the rest of the morning.

'For dinner we had roast lamb, mint sauce, roast and boiled potatoes, carrots and peas, followed by jam sponge and custard. (Today's football dieticians would surely have something to say about that!)

'More tough training in the afternoon is followed by another cooked meal at 5.30pm. Then local youngsters are put through 70 minutes of coaching and training. The players are officially free at 8.00pm and left winger 'Josser' Watling provides some entertainment by leading a sing song on a portable organ brought from Bristol.

'Tann's plan provides two week's concentrated training in which players 'live' soccer, open air recreation (cricket, golf, swimming), good and regular food, improved team work and team spirit which must come through living together, and great opportunities for young boys to improve their football.

'Disadvantages? I can't name any – except the cash outlay of about £350. It's cheap at the price.'

This photo takes us back to 1955 and Geoff Bradford, who had just learnt of his selection for England, is congratulated by Ray Warren, watched by Alfie Biggs, Jack Pitt, Ian Muir and Harry Bamford.

Bradford duly took his place in the England side that played Denmark, in Copenhagen, on 2nd October 1955. England won 5-1 and Bradford scored the final goal, eight minutes from time. He remains the only player to have been selected for England whilst still on Rovers' books.

He wasn't selected for his country again, but continued to find the back of the net for Rovers on a regular basis. His record of 242 goals in 461 league appearances speaks for itself, and it could have been more had he not suffered two serious leg injuries during his 15 years at Eastville.

Alfie Biggs was just 19 when the photo was taken, but had already made his first team debut and he also went on to score prolifically for the club, though fell short of Bradford's record, managing 178 goals in 424 appearances. His Eastville career was punctuated by a 15 month spell with Preston, for whom he scored 22 goals in 49 games, and he ended his career with spells at Walsall and Swansea.

Warren skippered the side regarded by many as the most successful in the club's history. Remarkably, he joined the club in 1935 and by the outbreak of the Second World War, had already made 69 first team appearances.

Jack Pitt, who died in 2004, aged 84, was 26 when he made his Rovers debut yet he went on to make 467 league appearances for the club. Another member of the successful 1950's side, Pitt also skippered the side for three seasons and was an ever-present on four occasions.

Pitt's great friend, Harry Bamford, was another stalwart of the 1950's side and his record of 486 appearances has been bettered only by Stuart Taylor. He had already made three appearances in the 1958/59 season, even though he was 38 and coming to the end of his career, when he died from injuries sustained in a road accident.

Ian Muir, whose father had also played for the club, found it difficult to break into the side, but was often selected as twelfth man, in the days before substitutes were allowed.. Although he made only 26 appearances in his four years at Eastville, he was a regular member of the reserve side. On leaving the club, he spent a season with Oldham before joining non-league outfit Rhyl.

Celebrating His England Call Up

The Card School

I'm unable to date this photo and can only confirm that it was taken between 1955 and 1958.

The man watching his charges play cards is Fred Ford, who arrived at Eastville in the summer of 1955 after five years as trainer at Carlisle.

The Londoner, who might well have represented his country had it not been for injury, played for Charlton, Millwall, Tottenham Hotspur and Carlisle and was, by all accounts, an uncompromising wing-half (a midfielder in today's world!).

He served in the Royal Engineers during the war, when he lost his index finger, and was mentioned in despatches.

His arrival in Bristol saw him link up with his great friend, Rovers boss Bert Tann, as coach. The two had been team-mates at Charlton and together they formed an excellent managerial team at Eastville.

He left in 1960, to take over as manager of Bristol City, a post he remained in until 1967, when he was relieved of his duties. After short spells as a coach with Torquay and Swindon, he returned to Eastville as manager, when Tann became general manager.

It was a short stay, as he took over as Swindon boss in August 1969. Another short spell as Torquay's coach followed his time at the County Ground and in 1981 he became Oxford United's Chief Scout, a position he held at the time of his death.

The card school here comprises of David Pyle, Dai Ward, Peter Sampson, Norman Sykes and Barrie Meyer. It would appear that a friendly game of cards was just that in those days, as there is a distinct lack of cash (or poker chips) on this table – maybe Fred was there to make sure that no one lost a packet!

Pyle, a central defender, signed for the club in 1955 and went on to make 139 league appearances before his move across the city to Ashton Gate in 1962.

Ward, a goalscoring inside-forward, who won two full international caps for Wales, ended his Rovers career with an astonishing haul of 90 goals in his 175 league appearances for the club.

Sampson was a stalwart of the side throughout the 1950s, making in excess of 300 league appearances, while Sykes had been an England Schoolboy and Youth international.

Meyer is probably better known for his career after football, that of county cricketer and Test umpire, though he was a useful footballer and turned out in 139 league games for Rovers and, like Pyle, also played for Bristol City.

Although this was obviously an informal gathering at someone's house, the dress code certainly wasn't casual! Everyone is wearing a suit or jacket and trousers, along with a collar and tie.

How times have changed!

I **have to say that this photo remains something of a mystery.**

There's no doubt who the players are: behind the kneeling figure of Howard Radford are Geoff Bradford, Barrie Meyer, Dai Ward, Paddy Hale, George Petherbridge, Geoff Fox and Peter Sampson.

The mystery is what they were doing, or about to do, at the time this photograph was taken. The most logical explanation, given that six of the players are sporting blazers with the club crest on the pocket, is that they were killing time whilst waiting to travel to an away game.

It's also difficult to put a date on the photo, though as Geoff Fox left the club in October 1955, and Paddy Hale signed his first professional contract with the club in February 1952, it was obviously taken some time between those dates.

Of the players shown, Bradford is obviously the most well known, and his career has been well documented over the years.

Meyer, who later found fame as an umpire in first class cricket, is also well know to followers of Bristol football, as he also played for City.

Welsh international Ward was a fiery inside-forward and he appears to be studying a newspaper quite closely, maybe looking for some racing tips for that particular day!

Hale spent a long time as understudy to Ray Warren during his time with the club, his most successful season, in terms of appearances, coming in 1957/58 when he appeared in

39 league games. Although a recognised central defender, he also stood in for Geoff Bradford at centre-forward in 1953/54 and scored 12 goals that season.

Petherbridge toured South Africa with an FA squad in 1956 and by the time his Rovers career came to an end he had appeared in 452 league games.

Fox was another stalwart of the Rovers side of the 1950s and was an ever-present in the promotion-winning side of 1952/53, as was Sampson. In fact, he was also ever-present in the season before, and after, that successful campaign and ended his Rovers career with 339 league appearances to his name.

Goalkeeper Radford also played his part in the 1952/53 promotion success, appearing in 10 games following the injuries sustained by regular custodian, Bert Hoyle, in a car accident. He went on to be a regular in the side in the first three seasons in the Second Division and appeared in a total of 244 league games for Rovers.

Which brings us full circle, still wondering where, when, and why, this photo was taken!

A Social Gathering?

The Harry Bamford Memorial Trophy

Already in this publication we have touched on the career of Harry Bamford and mentioned the fact that, following his death, the Harry Bamford Memorial Trophy established in his memory, was awarded each year to a deserving local sportsman.

He was highly thought of, both on and off the pitch, and was widely regarded as one of the finest players ever to represent Bristol Rovers.

The day after his death, on 31st October 1958, Rovers played Bristol City in a Second Division match at Eastville, a game that City won 2-1 in front of a crowd of 32,104.

The two Bristol clubs came together again at the end of that season, when a combined Bristol XI took on Arsenal in the Harry Bamford Memorial Match.

That game, also at Eastville, on 8th May 1959, also saw the first presentation of the Harry Bamford Memorial Trophy.

The first recipient was Bamford's Rovers colleague Geoff Bradford, who received the award from widow, Violet.

A photo of the presentation can be found in the Supporters Club Yearbook of 1959/60, along with many tributes to Bamford, although there is no interview with Bradford.

This photo shows Bradford handing over the trophy to the next recipient, Colin Mitchell, on 28th March 1960, following the prestigious friendly fixture against Swedish side Djurgarden.

Mitchell was, at the time, captain of Clifton St Vincents FC.

In the programme for that match it was stated that: *'Immediately after the game's conclusion the presentation of the trophy will be made and the first holder, Geoff Bradford, will be asked to present it to the Bristol Association Footballer who has been selected to receive the award for 1960.*

'The Committee making the selection consisted of the Chairman of the Gloucestershire Football Association, Bristol City FC and Bristol Rovers FC, together with the Sports Editors of the Evening Post, Evening World and the Western Daily Press.'

The trophy contained the following inscription:

'The Harry Bamford Memorial Trophy, presented annually to a player who has upheld the tradition of sportsmanship created by Harry Bamford, of Bristol Rovers FC, who died at the age of 38 on October 31st 1958.'

I believe that the award ceremony continued for a number of years and, amazingly, the Trophy has recently been found and is now on display in the club's administrative office.

The last recipient of the trophy, or at least the last name on the plinth, is that of R Bean of Soundwell who held it in 1973.

What happened to it between then and 2012 is anyone's guess, but at least it is now back with the club.

The 1961/62 season began with seven consecutive defeats and ended in relegation to the Third Division, following a nine-year stint in Division Two.

Bert Tann's side registered only 13 victories during the whole campaign, one of which came against Preston North End, at Eastville, on 24th February 1962. The game saw the former Rovers centre-forward Alfie Biggs return to his old stomping ground in the white shirt of his new club.

Biggs had scored the only goal of the game in the fixture between the clubs at Deepdale earlier in that season, and also scored in this game.

According the match report: 'An enthusiastic crowd cheered Rovers to a thrilling victory over Preston in the liveliest game seen at Eastville so far this season.

'The Eastville crowd gave former Rovers forward Alfie Biggs a rousing cheer as he led the Preston team on to the field.'

Local youngster Micky Slocombe came into the Rovers side in place of Norman Sykes, who was ruled out with an ankle injury.

Peter Hooper scored in the 22nd-minute to give Rovers the lead: 'Wylie fouled Jones 15 yards inside the Preston half. Bradford's free kick was neatly nodded forward by Mabbutt and Hooper, rushing in from the left, caught the ball on the bounce and headed it past Kelly.'

The visitors soon equalised: 'Radford rolled the ball out to Bumpstead but the right-half, caught on the hop, was quickly dispossessed by Spavin who pushed the ball to Dawson.

He chipped the ball back to Biggs who sent in a low angled drive from 10 yards outside the penalty area, which gave Radford no chance.

'But, a minute later, Rovers regained the lead with a goal by Bobby Jones. Again it was a Bradford centre which started the move. The ball was beautifully headed on to Jones by Williams and the inside-left chested it down before hooking it wide of Kelly.'

That goal, which turned out to be the winner, is shown in the photograph reproduced here. Geoff Bradford, playing at right-back (No 2) is to the right of the photo, while Keith Williams (No 8) is to the far left.

Rovers' number 4 is Dave Bumpstead and Ray Mabbutt is to the left of the goal, watching Bobby Jones hook the ball into the net with Harold Jarman (No 7) in close attendance.

Preston goalkeeper Kelly is almost hidden by Jones and the two outfield players are Wylie (No 4) and Smith (No 6).

There were no further goals in the second half, though Biggs almost scored a last-minute equaliser: '...with only Radford to beat he sent the ball well wide.'

A crowd of 10,601 saw this Rovers side in action: Radford, Bradford, Frowen, Bumpstead, Pyle, Slocombe, Jarman, Williams, Mabbutt, Jones, Hooper.

One Of The Thirteen

The Jones Boys

5-5 and Keith scored his goals as follows.

'On ten minutes he finished off a move started by Peter Hooper and continued by his namesake, Bobby. With 75 minutes on the clock he hit a shot that went in off the near post, and his third goal, after 83 minutes came when flicked the ball past Swindon goalkeeper O'Hara to complete the scoring for the evening.'

The next day, with the promise of a pro contract on the table, he travelled back to Wales to play his last game as an amateur for a Welsh FA XI against Combined Welsh Colleges at Ninian Park.

"I have always wanted to become a professional and have had other trials, but this certainly seems to be the best opportunity. This trial period with Rovers has been the most enjoyable I have had and I hope to make the grade," he said at the time.

However there was to be no happy ending as, in December 1962, his dream of a career in league football appeared to be over. The Green Un reported: *'Keith Jones is likely to leave Rovers next week. The former Welsh amateur international has been loaned to Gwynfi, a Rhondda Valley club near to his native Ton Pentre and played for them this afternoon.*

'Bert Tann's willingness to let Jones go is related to the current promise shown by Graham Muxworthy, Rovers other reserve outside-left, who has just returned from his National Service in Germany and the manager feels the 21-year-old Muxworthy is a better prospect than 25-year-old Jones.'

Rovers reserves lined up as follows that afternoon: Radford, Bradford, Frowen, Bumpstead, Pyle, Sykes, Jarman, Williams (K), Hooper, Jones (R), Jones (K).

Taken in August 1962, this photo features, from left to right, Keith, Gwyn and Bobby Jones. The trio were, no doubt, looking forward to the new campaign, Rovers' first back in the Third Division following relegation.

Bobby's career took in over 400 league games in two spells with the club he first joined in 1957. This was to be Gwyn's first season with the club following a move from Wolves for whom he had appeared in 21 league games, while Keith's Rovers career never really took off. In spite of that, though, he scored a hat-trick on his senior debut!

He had joined the club, from Ton Pentre, as an amateur triallist in 1961 and after a number of impressive reserve team performances, was given an opportunity to play in a first-team friendly at Swindon on Friday 26th January 1962.

Amazingly, there was a crowd of 3,939 in attendance for the game, and they were treated to a goals feast as it ended

This is a photo taken at the game played against Crystal Palace, at Eastville, on 25th August 1962.

It was the third game of the 1962/63 campaign and one that saw Rovers register their first win in their first season back in the Third Division.

The goals in a 2-0 win arrived courtesy of Harold Jarman and Keith Williams, and the game saw the debut of Allen Wood, who became the first amateur to play for Rovers in ten years. A 21-year-old Welsh amateur international, he had just completed his apprenticeship as a telecommunications engineer. He had been playing for Lovells Athletic and made his debut just two weeks after impressing in a trial match.

The first Rovers player to wear contact lenses, he was offered a professional contract after the Palace game, but that turned out to be his only league appearance for the club. He left Eastville in January 1963 and signed for Newport Athletic, for whom he made 156 league appearances in the next seven years.

The match report had this to say about his debut: '*New boy Allen Wood settled down well in the second half when the pressure was off, but in the first half gave little indication of remedying Rovers wing-half problem.*'

As for the game, it doesn't appear to have been a classic and it wasn't until the 75th minute that the crowd of 12,378 were treated to a goal: '*Collecting a pass just inside his own half, Jarman set off on a goalward jaunt which took him around three defenders. As he cut into the middle, Williams moved out to the wing to draw the full-back. Left with a clear view of goal,*

Jarman cracked in a low left-footed shot from just inside the Palace box and Glazier had no chance.'

A second goal arrived in the 89th minute: '*Williams, unlucky not to have scored earlier, headed Jarman's corner neatly inside the upright. McNichol handled the ball in a desperate bid to push it out, but only succeeded in helping it over his own line.*'

Williams and goalkeeper Esmond Million were implicated in a bribery scandal before the season was out and later banned from football for life. Rovers narrowly avoided a second successive relegation, beating Halifax Town in their penultimate game to guarantee their survival in Division Three.

This photo shows Jarman heading for goal, while the other Rovers players pictured (left to right) are Geoff Bradford, Terry Oldfield, Gwyn Jones (in the background) and Keith Williams.

The Rovers team that day was as follows: Million, Hillard, Jones (G), Wood, Sykes, Mabbutt, Jarman, Williams, Bradford, Oldfield, Jones (R).

First Third Division Victory

A Vital Two Points

This photo was taken on 14th May 1963, when Rovers entertained Colchester United at Eastville.

Goals from Geoff Bradford and Alfie Biggs sealed a 2-0 win, but the spectre of relegation to the Fourth Division still hung over the club: *'A 2-0 win against Colchester left Rovers needing two points from their final two games to avoid a second successive relegation.*

'They were worthy winners, but missed an opportunity of improving their goal difference, which could yet decide their fate.

'Sheer hard work and fighting spirit brought Rovers victory. Colchester were a skilful side, far more than Rovers, but a lack of urgency proved their undoing.'

The suspension of first-choice goalkeeper Esmond Million, for his part in the bribery scandal that rocked the football establishment, left the club short of cover for that very specialised position, though the press saw little cause for concern: *'Rovers should not have to look further than young Bernard Hall for a goalkeeper for next season. With Million suspended, he has stepped into the breach in fine style. He did not have a great deal to do but what he did was accomplished effortlessly, without blemish, and in good style.'*

Rovers took the lead after 34 minutes of the game, watched by a crowd of 9,004: *'A Biggs and Jones movement brought a penalty to Rovers, when McCrohan brought down Jones.*

'Biggs took the kick and blasted the ball high into the net.'

Roy McCrohan, whose foul led to the goal, had started his career at Reading before moving to Norwich, for whom he made 385 league appearances. He followed that up with 62 league games for Colchester before joining Rovers in August 1964. He played just 10 league games whilst at Eastville, all in the 1964/65 campaign.

The crucial second goal came after 69 minutes: *'Geoff Bradford moved into the middle to head a goal from a perfect centre by Hamilton. Much of the praise for this goal went to Biggs and Jones, who worked the ball through.'*

The photo shows Geoff Bradford trying to get in a cross despite the close attention of full-back Duncan Forbes. The Colchester player running back towards his own goal is McCrohan.

Rovers: Hall, Hillard, Jones (G), Oldfield, Davis, Mabbutt, Jarman, Jones (R), Biggs, Hamilton, Bradford.

Four days after beating Colchester, Rovers travelled to Halifax and picked up the two points they needed to avoid relegation, as they pulled off a famous 3-2 win at The Shay. It was just as well they won that one, as they suffered a 2-0 defeat at the hands of Port Vale in the last game of the season.

On 14th September 1963, Rovers faced Southend at Eastville, just three days after recording a 2-1 victory at Wrexham, their first of the 1963/64 campaign.

Alfie Biggs, who was to finish the season with 30 league goals, had scored once in that game and netted two more against Southend.

By all accounts, he was back to his best form: *'A hunger for goals has returned to the new club skipper and in the last few games he has shown he can still score in whatever position he is playing in.*

'The two he scored at Eastville on Saturday, against Southend, inspired Rovers first home win of the season and brought his total to five.'

The first of three goals in the opening 20 minutes arrived with nine minutes on the clock: 'Jones intercepted a bad back pass by Bradbury and switched the ball to Biggs who calmly placed it into the net with the goalkeeper well out of position.

'A minute later, Beesley nipped through a spreadeagled Rovers defence and neatly steered the ball past Hall.

'Then, on twenty minutes, shoot on sight Biggs restored Rovers lead with a fine header from a perfectly placed centre by Hillard.'

The goal of the game, though, was scored by Harold Jarman in the second half: *'Jarman revealed another side of his talent when he scored Rovers' third goal in the 54th minute with a searing low shot. Goy got his hands to the ball, but the sheer force behind it stretched his hands over the goal line.*

The referee, who was well up with play, had no hesitation in awarding a goal.

'Jarman almost hit a second goal with a similar effort during the final 20 minutes, when only the brilliance of goalkeeper Goy stopped Rovers from building up their lead.'

This photo shows the Southend keeper desperately trying to keep the ball out of the net, while Jarman can just be seen, in the centre of the photo, behind the more prominent figure of John Brown, while Bobby Jones is on the extreme right.

Brown was making his home debut for the club in this match, following a summer move from Plymouth Argyle, and while he was at the start of his Rovers career, Dave Bumpstead had reached the end of the road at Eastville.

The day before the Southend game, he was suspended for 14 days, after he had walked out saying he felt he had been unfairly dropped for a game against Oldham. He never played league football again, though he did later manage both Brentwood and Chelmsford City.

Watched by a crowd of 8,603, Rovers lined up as follows: Hall, Hillard, Jones (G), Oldfield, Davis, Mabbutt, Jarman, Jones (R), Biggs, Brown, Bradford.

Jarman's Gem!

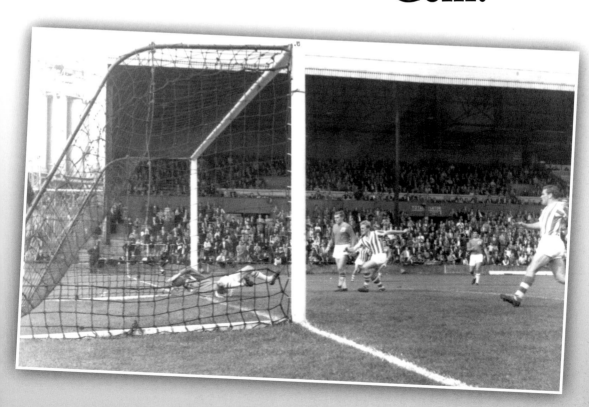

Rovers Win 50th Derby

This photo was taken at Eastville on 14th December 1963, when Rovers beat City 4-0 in the 50th league derby between the clubs.

Goalkeeper Bernard Hall, who was to make two vital saves from John Atyeo in the game, is seen here gathering a cross before it reaches the centre-forward, who is the only City player in the box.

Apart from Hall, the other Rovers players, from left to right, are Doug Hillard on the goal line, Gwyn Jones, Joe Davis next to Atyeo, John Brown, Ray Mabbutt and Terry Oldfield (No 4), while the other City player is Gordon Low.

Writing in the Evening Post, Robin Perry eloquently summed up the flavour of a derby day: *'All Bristol battles are in a category of their own. They are largely a contest of nerves in which a psychological superiority is normally translated into a practical victory.*

'The big testing time comes in the first few seconds after kick off. A dominance established then by one side, invariably causes panic in their opponents ranks.

'On Saturday Rovers, slipping into gear right from the start, produced their most impressive opening burst for a very long time. By the 11th minute a bewildered City defence had conceded three goals.'

The first goal arrived on four minutes, when goalkeeper Mike Gibson raced off his line to challenge Geoff Bradford as he raced on to a through ball from Hillard:

'The keeper lost possession of the ball and, in attempting to gather it again, pushed it over the goal-line. Bradford followed up to make sure, but the ball had already crossed the line.'

Goal number two arrived with nine minutes on the clock: *'Jarman shrugged off a tame tackle by Williams before rounding Thresher. This took him to the edge of the penalty area from where he hooked a low shot into the net off the far post with Gibson sprawling full length.'*

Two minutes later it was 3-0: *'Jarman's low free kick caught City's defence on the hop. Biggs was first to it, swung round, and volleyed a shot out of Gibson's reach.'*

There was one more goal to come, though it didn't arrive until the 85th minute: *'Bradford headed a superb goal. It was expertly taken from a beautifully judged pass. Hamilton, midway inside City's half, saw Bradford signal for the ball. He stroked it towards the far post as Bradford raced in and Gibson was left helpless as the left-winger headed into the back of the net.'*

It was Bradford's final goal for the club. He retired at the end of the season, his final appearance coming in the last home game, a 5-2 defeat at the hands of Reading.

A crowd of 19,451 saw these teams in action:

Rovers: Hall, Hillard, Jones (G), Oldfield, Davis, Mabbutt, Jarman, Brown, Biggs, Hamilton, Bradford.

City: Gibson, Briggs, Thresher, Parr, Connor, Low, Derrick, Clark, Atyeo, Williams, Hooper.

The photo below was taken on 18th September 1965 when Rovers, courtesy of a Bobby Jones hat-trick, beat Oxford United 3-1 at Eastville.

The consolation goal was scored by another player named Jones, Oxford's Tony.

Rovers, 5-1 winners against York in their previous game, kept the same side for this match against newly-promoted Oxford, and took the lead on 25 minutes.

'It was probably the best goal I've seen Bobby Jones score. Oldfield, pushed a square pass to Hillard, who had moved to the centre. The right-back stroked a low pass forward for Jones to take on the edge of the penalty area. The inside-left rolled the ball forward with his right foot, then pulled it back again to change feet, switched direction, which flummoxed the whole defence and hammered a low, left-foot drive past the helpless Fearnley.'

It took the visitors five minutes to equalise: *'Davis and Fearnley tangled on the touchline and Rovers' centre-half was penalised. Quartermain moved up to take the free kick halfway inside Rovers' half and curled over a centre.*

'There seemed a great deal of pushing and shoving in the goalmouth, but it was Tony Jones who finally got underneath the ball and headed it wide of Hall from close range.'

Rovers, though, took a lead into the half-time break, courtesy of a second Bobby Jones goal: *'It was a goal to which his skipper, Biggs, made a brilliant contribution. Jones darted forward through the middle, touched a pass to Biggs and streaked forward. Biggs held the ball, drew the defence, and then slipped it forward to Jones to take in his stride and hit it past the* advancing Fearnley from a sharp angle on the right.'

Jones completed his hat-trick in the 77th-minute: *'As with the first two goals it was his lightening speed, taking him past bewildered defenders, that earned him the opening.*

'As Jarman's centre came across, Jones controlled the ball neatly and tucked a low shot just inside the post.'

This Third Division fixture, watched by a crowd of 9,707, saw Rovers move into seventh place, with eight points from their opening seven games. Oxford were five places, but only one point, behind.

Neither side could mount a sustained promotion challenge, though, as Rovers finished in 16th position with Oxford just two places better off, though they would probably have been more satisfied at their placing given it was their first season at that level.

In this photo Jones, on the extreme right, appears to be hitting a left-foot shot past goalkeeper Fearnley. John Brown is the Rovers player nearest to Jones, while the closest Oxford player to him is Ron Atkinson.

Rovers: Hall, Hillard, Jones (G), Oldfield, Davis, Mabbutt, Jarman, Brown, Biggs, Jones (R), Munro.

Jones
The Goals!

Six Goals Shared With The Hammers

Pictured here is Harold Jarman, scoring Rovers' third goal in the 3-3 draw against West Ham in the first round of the League Cup on 21st September 1965.

Latecomers amongst the crowd of 18,354 would probably have missed the first West Ham goal, scored by Geoff Hurst after just two minutes.

Rovers were level on twenty minutes: *'With almost shy nonchalance, Johnny Brown unleashed a screaming left-foot shot from fully twenty yards that bulged the back of the net.'*

Hurst scored his, and West Ham's, second goal of the night just seven minutes later and only three more minutes had elapsed before Johnny Byrne added a third.

That wasn't the end of the first-half scoring, though, as Rovers pulled a goal back in the 42nd minute: *'Petts, lurking on the edge of the Hammers penalty area after a sweet left-wing move had temporarily broken down, lashed in a low drive which sped in off a post.'*

It took just five second-half minutes for Rovers to complete the scoring for the night: *'Petts started the move. Biggs touched the ball on to Jones on the left wing and the curving, curling, low centre eluded Biggs' outstretched boot but Jarman, charging past Burkett, stabbed the ball in.'*

The visitors, apparently, were fortunate to hold on and survived one particularly anxious moment: *'England U-23*

player Martin Peters slashed the ball past his own keeper in a moment of panic and for a fleeting second it seemed that this was going to be the fourth, and decisive, Rovers goal. But the ball struck the base of the post and bounced gently forward and the strolling players of a now ruffled First Division outfit scraped the ball clear.'

Manager Bert Tann was, according to press reports, in a buoyant mood afterwards: He had been reading his club's publicity propaganda, judging by his first comments after the match.

'Come to Eastville for entertainment. Everything happens at Eastville,' he said. *'And I defy anyone to disagree after this thrill-a-second League Cup game that earns from me a 10-star rating for entertainment value.*

'Rovers' largest crowd of the season witnessed what could well be the highlight of the club's season. Make no mistake about it West Ham, holders of the European Cup Winners Cup, and boasting five players capped for England in their ranks, came within an inch of defeat.'

The Hammers won the replay at Upton Park 3-2 eight days later and three members of their side – Moore, Peters and Hurst – won World Cup winners' medals in the summer of 1966.

Rovers: Hall, Hillard, Jones (G), Petts, Stone, Mabbutt, Jarman, Brown, Biggs, Jones (R), Munro.

Following a 3-1 defeat against Colchester at Layer Road the previous week, Rovers returned to Eastville on 17th September 1966, where they took on Swindon Town.

They ran out comfortable 3-0 winners thanks to goals from the 'H' squad of Hillard, Hamilton and 'H' himself, Harold Jarman who was making his 249th appearance for the club.

Taken at that match, this photo shows Doug Hillard in the foreground, looking as though he's failed to cut out a cross from Swindon's John Trollope, while Jarman looks on.

The first goal arrived after 24 minutes: *'Assisted by a marginal error of judgement by goalkeeper Downsborough, who carried the ball a foot too far outside his area. The linesman spotted him and Rovers were awarded a free kick smack in front of goal.*

'Hillard moved up to take it and blasted the ball into the net off the wall of the Swindon defenders positioned between himself and the goal.'

It was the only goal of the first half. Swindon did come close to equalising just before half-time but Bernard Hall produced a brilliant save to deny Dawson a goal.

Rovers increased their lead on 74 minutes with a controversial goa: *'A long pass out of defence found Jarman just over the halfway line. He looked several yards offside and the referee's whistle blew. But then it was realised that the injured Dawson was still standing alongside the goalkeeper, so referee Mr Burns allowed play to continue. Jarman moved into Swindon's penalty area, and took the ball round the advancing Downsborough.'*

Four minutes from time, the third goal of the afternoon arrived: *'Hamilton nipped in to steer a superb through pass from Jones wide of Downsborough, and slipped it into the net.'*

Press reports indicated that it was the side's best performance of the season to date and said: *'Rovers were full of blustering enthusiasm.'*

Victory saw the side move into second place in the Third Division table, with six points from nine games. League leaders at the time were Workington while Swindon were down in 17th place with four points from their six matches.

By the end of the season things had changed somewhat – particularly for Workington, who finished bottom.

Rovers ended the season in fifth place, just two points behind runners-up Middlesbrough, while Swindon were just three points and three places worse off.

A crowd of 10,907 saw this Rovers side in action: Hall, Hillard, Davis, Frude, Stone, Mabbutt, Jarman, Brown, Biggs, Hamilton, Jones.

The 'H' Squad Are On Target

Shock Cup Exit Avoided... Just!

This is a photo taken during the first round FA Cup tie between Oxford City and Rovers, played on 26th November 1966.

A crowd of 5,100 watched the match, played at the White House Ground that the non-league outfit leased from Brasenose College, Oxford. By the look of the photo it wasn't a bad little ground, though it's interesting to see the floodlight pylons emerging through the roof of the stand!

It has since disappeared under quite a few houses as it was sold off by the College in 1988 and Oxford City now play at Court Place Farm, where Rovers played a pre-season friendly fixture against them in 1999.

Back in 1966, Rovers were in second place in the Third Division while the amateurs of Oxford were seventh in the Isthmian League, though they were on a little bit of a roll, having won their previous five games.

Rovers found themselves two goals ahead early on and the opening paragraph of the match report read as follows: 'Christmas came a little bit early for Bristol Rovers this afternoon with Oxford City, their hosts and first round FA Cup opponents, presenting them with a couple of gifts, an own goal and a penalty, inside the first half-hour. It was a different story in the second half, with Oxford putting everything in as they bid to get a replay.'

The own goal came after 16 minutes: 'Oxford's lack of steadiness at crucial moments let them down as left-half John Lambert, showing the same tendency as his forwards to swing wildly at the ball, conceded an own goal. A chip through the middle by Ronaldson was meant for Jarman and Lamb intercepted, but sliced his clearance and lifted the ball over Shipperley's head.

'After the keeper had saved well from Jarman, Rovers increased their lead from the penalty spot. Rashness on the ball again brought advantage to Rovers, as Jackson plunged and tripped Munro just inside the area and Joe Davis drove the kick low and decisively wide of Shippey.'

The amateurs hit back after the break: 'On 65 minutes, a sudden Oxford breakaway brought a goal. John Woodley, rounding Taylor with consummate ease on the edge of the penalty area, strode on and beat Hall with a powerful drive.'

Five minutes later, the home side were level: 'The game had been strangely short of atmosphere. But not now. The pitch was invaded by jubilant youngsters almost before Tony Bradbury's shot had reached the net.'

The replay, three days later at Eastville, saw Rovers register a comfortable 4-0 win.

Rovers: Hall, Davis, Parsons, Stone, Taylor, Mabbutt, Jarman, Brown (J), Biggs, Ronaldson, Munro.

Pictured in the True Blue Club at Eastville, on 25th August 1967, are Alex Munro, Lindsay Parsons, Ian Hamilton, Bobby Jones, Harold Jarman and Ronnie Briggs.

The reason for the gathering in the bar at the club is not immediately obvious, but as Bobby Jones had rejoined Rovers the previous day, I think it's safe to assume that the photo was taken to mark his return to the club.

It is to be hoped that the players refrained from partaking of the well-stocked bar on this occasion, as they had a home game against Colchester United the next day!

Munro, who scored from the penalty spot in the 1-1 draw the following afternoon, was a Scot who signed for Rovers in September 1962 and went on to make 168 league appearances in almost ten years at Eastville.

Parsons, on the other hand, graduated through the ranks and was a first-team regular for more than a decade. He ended his Rovers career with 358 league appearances to his name.

He later played for Torquay and a number of local non-league clubs before becoming manager of Cheltenham Town. Still involved in the game, he has worked at a number of clubs with another former Rovers player, Tony Pulis, and the pair are currently working together at Stoke City.

Hamilton, the only one of the five players featured here who didn't play the following day, scored 60 goals in 149 league appearances for Rovers in an Eastville career spanning ten years. That total would, in all probability, have been a lot higher had it not been for the knee injuries that dogged his career.

Only eight players have made more league appearances for the club than the 421 that Bobby Jones has to his name, and only four players have scored more than his 101 league goals. Both totals might have been higher had he not spent the best part of a year away from Eastville following his transfer to Northampton in September 1966 and subsequent move to Swindon in February 1967.

Jarman was one of the players who beat Bob's appearance and goals total. He notched 127 goals in 452 league games and was a talented footballer who also played first class cricket for Gloucestershire between 1961 and 1971.

Goalkeeper Briggs played only 35 league games for Rovers, but was a very talented keeper who joined Manchester United in 1960 when he shared digs with George Best. Capped at Schoolboy and U-23 level by Northern Ireland, he also won two full caps for his country.

The side that faced Colchester the next day, in front of a crowd of 8,260, was: Briggs, Mabbutt, Parsons, Williams (J), Taylor (S), Munro, Jarman, Frude Biggs, Jones (W), Jones (R).

Bobby's Return

Rovers And City Combine

Although he recovered from the injury, his football career was over after 163 first team appearances.

His had made his debut on Good Friday 1962, in a 2-2 draw against Charlton Athletic, and when a bribery scandal involving regular first-team goalkeeper Esmond Million broke a year later, Hall assumed the mantle of first-choice keeper.

I believe it was only the second time in Bristol football history that a combined Rovers and City side had played a match. The previous occasion was in 1959 when the two clubs combined to play Arsenal in a benefit game for the relatives of Rovers' full-back Harry Bamford, who had died as a result of injuries sustained in a road accident.

The testimonial brochure acknowledged the help and support received from City, and Rovers' chairman Philip Hort said: *'We appreciate very much the co-operation of Bristol City Football Club in allowing their players to take part in the match and also agreeing to the sale of the brochure at Ashton Gate.'*

A crowd of almost 9,000 turned out for the game and as the teams emerged from the dressing rooms, they lined up either side of the tunnel, allowing Hall to walk between them on to the pitch. He was met by O'Rourke, who stepped forward to shake his hand before taking him to meet Hammers' skipper Bobby Moore.

The Hammers won 4-3, thanks to goals from Peter Brabrook, Harry Redknapp, Geoff Hurst and John Sissons, while Rovers replied with an own goal from Kitchener and goals from Ken Ronaldson and Jarman.

Combined Bristol XI: Gibson, Hillard, Briggs, Williams (J), Connor, Quigley, Jarman, Ronaldson, O'Rourke (Biggs), Crowe, Jones (R).

West Ham: Ferguson (Grotier), Charles, Kitchener, Peters, Bonds, Moore, Redknapp, Boyce, Brabrook, Hurst (Bennett), Sissons.

Ibelieve that this photo was taken a few days before Bernard Hall's testimonial match on 16th October 1967, for the team photo on the centre spread of his testimonial brochure.

A combined Bristol side took on West Ham, and City players Gordon Low, Hugh McIlmoyle and Lou Peters, are pictured with Wayne Jones, Stuart Taylor, Dave Stone, Doug Hillard and Harold Jarman, apparently waiting to be called into the photo.

The three City players pictured never played in the match, but five of their colleagues did – Mike Gibson, Alec Briggs, Jack Connor, John Quigley and Chris Crowe.

Hall, Rovers' 25-year-old goalkeeper, had been injured in the last game of 1966, when Rovers took on Middlesbrough at Eastville.

A 54th minute collision with visiting centre-forward John O'Rourke resulted in him being rushed to Frenchay Hospital, where he remained unconscious for 16 days.

Having beaten non-league sides Arnold and Wimbledon in the first and second rounds of the 1967/68 FA Cup, Rovers were handed a third round tie against Bristol City at Ashton Gate.

This photo is from that match, played on 27th January 1968, and shows Alfie Biggs being challenged by City's Alec Briggs on the extreme left of the photo. Bobby Jones is the closest Rovers player to Biggs, while the three City players are Gordon Parr, Terry Bush and Jack Connor. Harold Jarman is the Rovers player on the far right.

Third Division Rovers were the underdogs against a City side who were in Division Two at the time though, by all accounts, it was a drab game.

'Against all the odds, Rovers held City in Bristol's big cup tie at Ashton Gate. But the strangely subdued, goal-less, encounter must have sent supporters of both teams home with a feeling of anti-climax.

'There was no atmosphere before the game, despite the big crowd, who had paid a record near-£10,000 to see the cup tie and there was nothing in a pedestrian first half to raise the temperature of even the most excitable of fans.'

The opening 45 minutes were, apparently, largely uneventful and the best chance fell to Rovers – but after Jones was fouled by Parr, the winger saw his free kick cleared by the home defence. Apart from Wayne Jones driving a shot across the face of City's goal, that was as good at it got for the crowd of 37,237.

It wasn't a lot better in the second half, but: *'The first five minutes were played almost exclusively in the City half and it was Bobby Jones causing the damage.*

'Gibson dived to hold a cross from him and then he was halted by Briggs on the edge of the area.'

As for City, Crowe saw a free kick blocked before they squandered an opportunity to take the lead. *'Clever work by Crowe, followed by a through pass to the forward-moving Galley enabled City's leading scorer to get in a fierce right-foot shot, but Taylor went to his left to keep the ball out.'*

Gibson saved from Jones before the final whistle, but the draw meant a replay at Eastville on the following Tuesday, when 30,257 fans saw City go through to round four courtesy of a 2-1 win.

Over at Eastville, on the same day as the cup tie, Rovers reserves hosted their City counterparts in a Football Combination match. City ran out 4-1 winners thanks to goals from Sharpe (2), Low and Bartley, while Ray Graydon was on target for Rovers.

Rovers finished the season in 16th place in the Third Division, while City, whose cup run ended in the fifth round with a 2-0 defeat at Leeds, finished 19th in the Second Division.

The teams at Ashton Gate lined up as follows.

Rovers: Taylor (L), Hillard, Munro, Williams (J), Taylor (S), Stone, Jarman, Jones (W), Biggs, Mabbutt, Jones (R)

City: Gibson, Parr, Briggs, Wimshurst, Connor, Bush, Derrick, Crowe, Galley, Quigley, Peters.

City Stalemate

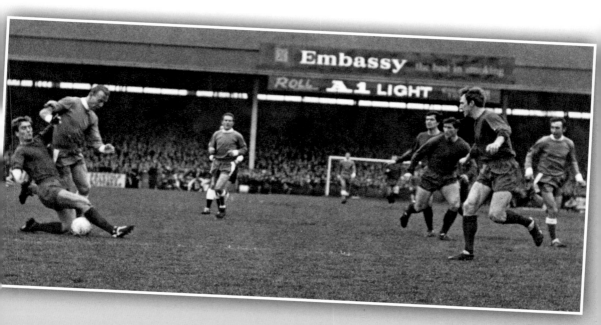

Table Toppers!

Providing a specific date for this photo has been difficult, and all I can tell you is that it was probably taken in 1968 after Fred Ford had taken over as manager and Bert Tann had become general manager.

Bobby Jones, on the extreme left of the photo, is taking on Tann at table football, watched by Ford and Bobby Campbell, a future Rovers boss, and Doug Hillard.

Jones was in his second spell at the club, having returned to Eastville in the summer of 1967 after brief stints at Northampton and Swindon.

Ford had been a team-mate of Tann at Charlton Athletic before the Second World War, and the two were reunited in 1955 when he arrived at Eastville as coach.

He was manager of Bristol City from 1960 to 1967 and then managed Rovers and Swindon before enjoying a long association with Oxford United, where he was chief scout at the time of his death in 1981.

Campbell won five full caps for Scotland following his move to Chelsea in 1947, and he remained at Stamford Bridge until 1954, when he joined Reading.

He came to Rovers in 1961 as first-team coach, and was manager of the club between 1967 and 1969.

Hillard first joined Rovers in 1957 and by the time he left Eastville 11 years later, he had made a total of 318 league appearances for the club.

For a decade he was the regular choice at right-back and he was ever-present in seasons 1963/64 and 1965/66.

Club honours eluded him as the Rovers side of the 1950s were on the wane by the time he made his debut in 1958/59, and he was at the club when they were relegated to the Third Division in 1962, though he only played seven games that season because of a broken leg.

However, on his return to full fitness he again became a regular in the first team and was Player of the Year on two occasions.

As for Tann, a couple of sentences hardly do justice to the man in charge of the club throughout the 1950s. In all, he was manager for 18 years and general manager from 1968 until his death, at the age of 58, in 1972.

In spite of being restricted by a 'No Buy, No Sell' policy, he led his side to two FA Cup quarter-finals and two sixth-place finishes in the Second Division, coming very close to leading his charges into the promised land that was then Division One.

The date shown on the reverse of this photo is 10th December 1968.

Quite why it was taken is anyone's guess, the most obvious explanation being that the local press were out to promote the club's second round FA Cup replay against Bournemouth at Eastville that evening.

The photo shows trainer Bobby Campbell seemingly checking what studs Bobby Jones, Ray Graydon, Wayne Jones, Ray Mabbutt and Harold Jarman were going to use for the game.

Fred Ford's side had beaten Peterborough 3-1 at Eastville in the first round of that season's competition, then played out a goal-less draw against Bournemouth at Dean Court. They progressed to the third round three days later after Graydon scored the only goal of the game, so he obviously chose the right boots!

The goal came after just two minutes: *'Bolton fouled Wayne Jones out on Rovers left wing. Tom Stanton took the free kick, which curved in towards Bournemouth's goal.*

'Stuart Taylor had moved up and it was his imposing presence in the penalty area that occupied the attention of most defenders.

'Graydon saw his chance and darted across from the right to meet the ball just in front of a waiting Roger Jones and headed it past the keeper from close range.'

Rovers had chances to add to their lead during the first half: *'Graydon blasted the ball on to a post after Ray Mabbutt's header had been blocked, Bobby Jones passed to Mabbutt instead of shooting when well placed, Mabbutt headed over the bar, and Graydon saw his header saved.'*

Bournemouth did get the ball into the net three minutes into the second half, but the effort was ruled out as the scorer, Hold, was in an offside position. Goalkeeper Laurie Taylor saved efforts from Powell and Hold before Rovers threatened again, though they were unable to score a second goal.

The win enhanced manager Ford's record in the FA Cup: *'His proud record of never having failed to get his team into the third round since he first became a manager, in 1960, remains intact.*

'There were moments of good football, individual and collective; some sterling defensive work, particularly by Rovers' giant twin centre-halves Taylor and Larry Lloyd, and a workrate throughout the side that completely knocked Bournemouth out of their stride in the first half.'

The win, watched by Rovers' biggest crowd of the season to date, 11,898, earned them a third round tie against Kettering.

Rovers: Taylor (L), Parsons, Stanton, Taylor (S), Lloyd, Petts, Graydon, Jones (R), Mabbutt, Jones (W), Jarman. Substitute: Ronaldson.

Choosing The Right Footwear

Lowest Post-War League Crowd

In this photo, Bobby Jones takes on a Southport defender in the Third Division match played at Eastville on 30th November 1968.

Jones scored both Rovers' goals in a 2-1 win, watched by a crowd of 4,768, in conditions that weren't the best.

'Bristol Rovers, in urgent need of points, took a 40th minute lead through a Bobby Jones penalty at mud-bound Eastville this afternoon, after Southport had started off the more dangerous side.

'The Eastville pitch survived the recent heavy rain remarkably well. Rain was still falling steadily when the game started, and although the ground obviously was extremely heavy, there was no surface water.

'If the rain was not bad enough to cause a postponement, it was certainly bad enough to keep supporters away, and the meagre crowd looked certain to be enough to be Eastville's lowest post-war attendance for a league match.' (It was!)

The opening goal came five minutes before half-time when Rovers, kicking towards the Tote End, won a penalty: *'Jarman cut in from the left and, as he chipped over a centre, the ball was beaten down by Alex Russell.'*

'There were many who thought that the defender was merely trying to protect his face but, despite the Southport protests, the referee and linesman agreed a penalty. Jones hit a low kick to Armstrong's left as the keeper moved to dive in the opposite direction.'

It was a lead that Rovers kept until the 65th minute: *'Mabbutt burst through on a telling pass from Wayne Jones and rounded Malcolm Russell, but clashed with Armstrong before he could get in a shot.*

'The ball was scrambled away and, as Mabbutt lay injured, Southport moved upfield to snatch an equaliser, Andrews heading in a right-wing centre by Harkin from close range.'

Mabbutt was unable to continue and was replaced by Ken Ronaldson and it was his pass that led to a second goal for Rovers, and for Bobby Jones: *'Ronaldson provided a perfect left-wing centre for Bobby Jones to turn past Armstrong with a hooked shot.'*

It was a lead that they held until the final whistle. Although the visitors pressed hard for a second equalising goal, the closest they came to getting it was when Andrews sliced his shot, from a cross by Fields, and the ball was scrambled away by a grateful Rovers defence.

The win saw Rovers move into 14th place with 18 points from their 20 games, whilst Southport were three places and one point worse off.

Rovers lined up as follows that day: Taylor (L), Parsons, Stanton, Taylor (S), Lloyd, Petts, Graydon, Jones (R), Mabbutt (Ronaldson), Jones (W), Jarman.

Having suffered their first defeat of the 1969/70 season at Luton a week before, Rovers returned to winning ways against Fulham on 13th September 1969.

The game was billed as the 'Day of the Dodgins' as Bill senior was in charge of Rovers, while his son, Bill junior, was the Fulham manager.

However they were upstaged by Harold Jarman, pictured here slotting home a penalty in Rovers 3-2 win, whose goal saw him enter the record books.

A road accident meant that Fulham arrived at Eastville less than 30 minutes before kick off, though that didn't appear to affect them in any way, and the game burst to life midway through the first half with three goals in as many minutes.

On 23 minutes: *'Jimmy Conway led the attack, bursting forward down the right, giving a wall pass to Barrett and streaking forward to take the immediate return. He beat Sheppard inside the near post with a low drive hit on the run.*

'Two minutes later Rovers were on level terms. It was a goal all the Rovers fans wanted to see – Harold Jarman's 111th, bringing the skipper the club's scoring record for a winger in his 400th first-team appearance.

'Seymour plunged courageously to save at Stubbs' feet and the ball spun out to Jarman who was way out to the right. He glided round Brown and was pulling away when the Fulham left-back brought him down three yards inside the area.

'It was a nerve-wracking moment for Jarman, but his class came through as he beat Seymour with a spot kick driven high to the goalkeeper's right.'

Within a minute, though, Fulham had regained the lead: *'The offside trap went wrong and Rovers' defence was stretched out across the field when Gilchrist hit a long ball out of defence down Fulham's right wing.*

'Earle, at first glance, looked offside, but over on the opposite flank Roberts was a couple of yards behind the rest of his defenders. The linesman's flag stayed down and Earle ran on to beat the advancing Sheppard with a low shot on the run.'

Two minutes into the second half, Rovers equalised: *'There seemed little danger to Fulham's goal when Gilchrist turned the ball back towards his own keeper from the right-hand edge of the area.*

'Stubbs anticipated the pass, sprinted forward, beat the onrushing Seymour to the ball and chipped it into the net from an acute angle.'

The winning goal arrived just after the hour: *'Wayne Jones, moving forward in an inside-left position, hit a cross pass into Fulham's penalty area. Graydon, moving in off the right, met the ball on the run, deflecting it just inside the post with his toe.'*

A crowd of 10,633 saw Rovers line up as follows: Sheppard, Roberts, Parsons, Marsland, Taylor, Munro, Graydon, Jones (W), Stubbs, Jones (R), Jarman. Substitute: Stanton.

A Place In The Record Books

A High Scoring Draw

Newport County striker Tony Buck equalised for the visitors: *'Rochdale launched a quick attack down the right, Butler pulling back a centre for Buck to hammer past Sheppard with a ferocious first-time left-footed shot.'*

There were no further goals in the first half, but Rochdale took the lead 12 minutes into the second period, after Harker had denied Jarman his second goal of the afternoon with a superb save.

'Buck dashed in on the near post to meet Rudd's right-wing centre and power the ball past Sheppard with his head.'

Rovers hit back though, and two goals in the space of three minutes appeared to have given them victory: *'Stubbs weaved his way through to beat Harker with a shot off the foot of a defender.'*

That goal came in the 78th minute and then, with the reporter obviously preparing to file his copy, this happened: *'Bobby Jones spurted through a gap, drew goalkeeper Harker and, showing fine control, guided the ball into the net.'*

So, with the report of the match finished, and Rovers leading 3-2, it was all ready to go when the visitors scored a dramatic late equaliser. There was no time for a massive rewrite, just a change to the opening paragraph and headline and a hurriedly written final paragraph: *'With the game in the third minute of injury time, Buck completed his hat-trick to give Rochdale a well deserved point.'*

The point gained by Rovers saw them move up to tenth place in the Third Division table, with 12 points from 10 games. Rovers: Sheppard, Roberts, Parsons, Prince, Taylor, Munro, Graydon, Jones (W), Stubbs, Jones (R), Jarman. Substitute (not used): Marsland.

This photo was taken on 27th September 1969 when Rovers and Rochdale played out a 3-3 draw at Eastville, watched by a crowd of 8,652.

Robin Stubbs and Harold Jarman are the two Rovers players closing in on goalkeeper Chris Harker as he just manages to hold on to a cross, while full-back Graham Smith guards the net.

The game was described in the following way in the local press: *'In a game of dramatically fluctuating fortunes Rovers and Rochdale, the best team to visit Eastville this season, finished all square.'*

The crowd didn't have too long to wait for the first goal, which came from the penalty spot after just 11 minutes: *'Stubbs set off again through the middle. He dribbled past Ashworth, then around Ryder and finally Parry to pull clear of Rochale's defence.*

'But Parry stretched out a leg, bringing Stubbs down from behind. The penalty decision was automatic.

'Jarman beat Harker with a kick driven high to the goalkeeper's right.'

Rovers held the lead for just five minutes when the former

Rovers went into their Third Division fixture against Bradford City on 22nd November 1969 hoping to get back to winning ways after suffering successive 3-1 defeats at the hands of Shrewsbury Town and Doncaster Rovers respectively.

They didn't quite manage it though, and had to be content with a 1-1 draw. Harold Jarman is pictured scoring the opening goal of the game. Bobby Jones, hoping to score his 100th goal for the club, was unable to join him on the scoresheet.

The opening paragraph of the match report said: *'Rovers were often in trouble against Bradford City's efficient side. With their defence often uncertain and their wing-halves failing to command the midfield, Rovers were well below their best. But they still would have built a commanding lead had it not been for some great goalkeeping by Pat Liney.'*

Rovers, playing against the side with the best defensive record in the division, went in search of an early goal and it arrived with just five minutes on the clock: *'The move started as Stanton sent Graydon away down the right wing. His centre was nodded down by Stubbs for Jarman to hit on the turn and lash high into the corner of the goal with his right foot.'*

The visitors went close to scoring through Corner and Ham before they equalised on the half-hour mark: *'Middleton scored at the end of a swift attack, which sliced an unimpressive looking Rovers defence wide open. The move started from Hallett, who sent Ham streaking down the right. A hard-driven centre square*

across the face of goal was taken in his stride by Middleton, who forced the ball home from close range.'

There were no further goals, though after the break Ham was always a danger for the visitors. Rovers, though, and Stubbs in particular, enjoyed a purple patch in the second period and the Rovers striker was only denied a goal by three excellent saves from Liney.

A crowd of 8,986 saw this Rovers side in action: Taylor (L), Stanton, Parsons, Roberts, Taylor (S), Prince, Graydon, Jones (W), Stubbs, Jones (R) (Brown, 74), Jarman.

In the week leading up to the game, Rovers boss Bill Dodgin had said he was recommending a Rovers half-back line of Jeff Coombs, Alan Impey and Peter Aitken to the Welsh FA who were fielding a professional youth side for the first time that season: *"It's a ready-made half-back line and there can't be many Welsh youngsters about who can better these three,"* said the manager.

It was also reported that Rovers were giving a trial to Aberdeen teenager Mitchell Knight – wonder what happened to him?

A Share Of The Spoils

Five Score Fifty

My guess is that this photo was taken just before the start of the 1969/70 season.

This is based only on the fact that the shirts worn by the players are complemented by white shorts, and socks the same colour as the shirts. At the start of the following season, the club switched to wearing white socks.

It was also the first season that Robin Stubbs, pictured in the centre of the five players, was with the club, following a summer move from Torquay United.

On the extreme left of the photo is Ray Graydon, and next to him is Wayne Jones. Harold Jarman is on the extreme right, with Bobby Jones next to him. The five of them played in the forward line on a number of occasions that season, and scored 50 league goals between them.

It was a season when Rovers finished third, behind runners-up Luton and champions Orient. Had they won their final two games of the season, they would have gained promotion themselves, but a 2-1 home defeat at the hands of Gillingham and a 5-2 loss at Tranmere kept them in the Third Division, where they were to remain until 1974.

Stubbs was brought to the club by new manager Bill Dodgin, a surprise choice as boss following Fred Ford's departure to Swindon.

Dodgin was a believer in attacking football, so the signing of a player with an impeccable goalscoring record came as no surprise.

Stubbs had moved to Torquay, from Birmingham, in 1972 and in two spells with the club he amassed a total of 122 goals in 233 league games, finishing as the club's top scorer on five occasions.

He managed that feat twice for Rovers, ending the 1969/70 campaign with 15 to his name and bettered that by two the following season.

The four players pictured with Stubbs, knocking goals into the goal at the Muller Road end at Eastville, with the Tote End in the background, will need no introduction.

Graydon went on to become a League Cup winner with Aston Villa and also played for Coventry. He enjoyed a stint in America, with Washington Diplomats, before embarking on a coaching career with Oxford and Southampton. Following time as manager of Walsall, he returned, in April 2002, for a less-than-successful spell as manager of the club where it all began for him.

Wayne Jones was already a full Welsh international with over 200 games for Rovers behind him when he was forced to retire from the game in 1972. He subsequently qualified as a physiotherapist and has worked for a number of clubs in that capacity.

Bobby Jones was a prolific goalscorer, amassing 101 league goals for Rovers. He scored eight in the near-miss season of 1969/70, while Jarman scored 127 in his Rovers career, and notched ten in the season in question.

This photo was taken on 14th April 1970 when Rovers took on Gillingham at Eastville, needing a win to maintain their promotion challenge.

Prior to the game, their penultimate Third Division fixture, they occupied second place with two games to play and were two points behind leaders Orient and a point ahead of third-placed Luton, though both of those clubs had three games to play.

However ,they blew their chance of promotion: *'Oh Rovers, what a boob!'* read the opening line of the match report and it continued: *'A crowd of 18,978 turned up at Eastville last night, confident of seeing them move two points nearer promotion at the expense of third from bottom Gillingham.*

'But Gills, on the defensive for 95% of the game, plundered a victory that gives them hope of avoiding the drop to the Fourth Division.'

Rovers couldn't have made a better start to the game, opening their account after just 43 seconds: *'Phil Roberts, by far the night's outstanding player, started the move with a fine long pass which Robin Stubbs headed inside to Wayne Jones.*

'His clipped forward pass found Sandy Allan, who rounded one defender and drove in a 25-yard shot which dipped under the bar after beating a surprised John Simpson five yards out from his line.'

Although Allan twice went close to increasing the lead and Wayne Jones hit a shot into the side netting, it seems that Rovers looked far from comfortable against their visitors.

The equalising goal came after 23 minutes: *'Former Yeovil forward Ken Pound rounded a stumbling Don Megson and the same player scored for a second time just after half-time when he left Tony Ford stranded and outstripped Stuart Taylor and Roberts to beat Dick Sheppard with a low shot slotted just inside the far post.'*

Three minutes after replacing Allen, substitute Carl Gilbert, a former Gillingham player, headed against the bar and Rovers then went close to scoring again: *'David Quirk stuck out a leg to deflect a shot from Peter Higgins wide. Megson rushed in and the crowd cheered an equaliser before they realised the ball had gone into the side netting.'*

'Wayne Jones was denied a goal by a save which Simpson knew little about and Gillingham, who played for a point, went away with two.'

Rovers boss Bill Dodgin said afterwards: *"It was the biggest disappointment of my life in football. I felt sick for myself, for the lads, for everyone in the club and, most of all, for the supporters.*

"I thought they were terrific. I know I've said some things about the Bristol fans in the past, but the way they took the disappointment of this game brought a lump to my throat. And that is a feeling I have rarely experienced."

Rovers: Sheppard, Ford, Megson, Roberts, Taylor, Jones (B), Jarman, Jones (W), Stubbs, Allan (Gilbert, 52), Higgins.

Promotion Hopes Disappear

Liverpool Turn Out for Harold

It was on 20th April 1970 that Liverpool arrived at Eastville to provide the opposition for Harold Jarman's testimonial match.

Taken during that game, this photo shows Harold having a quiet word with goalkeeper Ray Clemence. Judging by the reaction of the Rovers player in the background (Frankie Prince, I believe), it was taken just after Rovers had scored.

Before the match Jarman, the holder of the Harry Bamford Memorial Trophy, presented the trophy to Bristol City's Terry Bush.

The game was watched by a crowd of 6,676, and ended 1-1. Bobby Jones scored for Rovers, while Ian St John equalised for the visitors.

Jarman's testimonial programme included a number of glowing tributes to the winger who scored 127 goals in 452 league appearances for Rovers and his manager Bert Tann had this to say: *'To those followers of the game who place skills of ball control, close possession, accuracy of pass, added to goal scoring flair, above all the other important but more mundane assets, like work rate and physical football, known in days of yore as 'getting stuck in' Harold Jarman has given great delight for a number of seasons.'*

Local journalist Robin Perry summed up Jarman's time at Eastville as follows: *'...what a much duller decade the sixties would have been for the Rovers had it not been for Harold Jarman.'*

As for the report of the game against the men from Anfield, the local press said: *'The results of such encounters have little meaning. But when spirits had sunk so low after the defeats by Gillingham and Tranmere, a clash with a side as efficient as Liverpool presented an opportunity for the players to restore some of their lost confidence.'*

The games referred to were the final league matches of the 1969/70 campaign when defeats consigned Rovers to another season of Third Division football when, for so long, it seemed as though they would be promoted.

The game saw the return to Eastville of former central defender Larry Lloyd, who had moved to Anfield the previous summer after just one season of league football in Rovers' colours: *'It was not quite the homecoming Larry Lloyd had in mind. The £50,000 Rovers export, Liverpool's skipper for the night, was badly at fault when Bob Jones eased past him to slide in a Frankie Prince pass after just 21 minutes.*

'Rovers stayed in front until the 40th minute when Ian St John, who earlier had a goal disallowed for offside, equalised from Brian Hall's pass.'

Three Rovers players appear to have shone in the game: *'Jones hit the inside of a post, Prince played well and Parsons covered and tackled immaculately.'*

Rovers: Sheppard, Ford, Parsons, Roberts, Taylor, Prince, Graydon, Jones (W), Gilbert, Jones (R), Jarman. Substitute: Higgins.

Rovers took on Newcastle United at Eastville in the second round of the League Cup on 8th September 1970.

The home side had to make a change to their starting line-up ahead of the match: *'Carl Gilbert, idol of the Tote End fans, leads the Bristol Rovers attack, deputising for joint leading scorer Robin Stubbs, who failed a fitness test on his twisted knee and misses his first game of the season.'*

First Division Newcastle, who had won their previous two away games, travelled down to the area the day before the game and held a light training session at their Weston-super-Mare base on the morning of the match.

Bobby Jones scored twice to give Rovers a comfortable lead going into the final minutes: *'The result was flattering to Newcastle. Their goal was scored in injury time by Keith Dyson and never had any chance of influencing the game's outcome.'*

The headlines belonged to Jones, and this was what the papers had to say afterwards: *'It wasn't just a flash in the pan that has made Bobby Jones the toast of Bristol football today. It's taken a lot of hard work and determination for him to climb back to the top of the Eastville ladder.*

'And last night, when his two goals crushed mighty Newcastle United to put Rovers in the third round of the League Cup, was his reward.'

Jones said: *"I knew that I wouldn't be in the side for the start of the season, and began to push a bit harder. I did extra training and trimmed down to 5lbs lighter than I've ever been.*

"But I don't think I ever thought it would all end up quite as well as this."

His goals were described as follows: *'His first, a running header from Ray Graydon's right-wing centre, came two minutes before half-time. His second, a sharp piece of opportunism which exploited not the first moment of indecision by Ollie Burton, was scored six minutes after the restart.*

'What should have been his third, on 59 minutes, was a Sheppard clearance helped on to him by Carl Gilbert, but Jones lashed his shot on to goalkeeper Liam McFaul's chest.'

Of that chance Jones commented: *"I was too close to get an angle, but it still should have been a goal."*

Newcastle boss Joe Harvey said: *"Rovers played as if they wanted to win the League Cup, and we didn't."*

Our photo shows Jones wheeling away after scoring for Rovers, while goalkeeper Liam McFaul can only watch the net bulge and central defender Bobby Moncur (No 5) is also a spectator.

Rovers: Sheppard, Roberts, Parsons, Jones (B), Taylor, Megson, Graydon, Jones (R), Gilbert, Jones (W), Jarman. Substitute (not used): Higgins.

Newcastle Dumped Out Of The Cup

Extra Time Victory

In 1970/71, on their way to a Quarter Final appearance in the League Cup, Rovers came up against Norwich City in the third round.

A 1-1 draw at Carrow Road was followed by a 3-1 win, after extra time, in the replay at Eastville and our photo shows Harold Jarman in action during that match, which was played on 13th October 1970.

Second Division Norwich were missing the injured trio of Malcolm Darling, Max Briggs and Peter Silvester and gave 17-year-old Glen Self his first-team debut, just a few days after he'd scored in a reserve team fixture at Eastville.

The report of the game suggests that Rovers were on top once the whistle had blown for the start of the second half: *'If ever the just triumphed over the unjust on the football field, it was at Eastville last night in a fantastic game of high drama.*

'Afterwards the stadium's biggest crowd of the season, 19,122 of them, rose to acclaim a superhuman effort by Rovers during the second half and throughout the half hour of extra time.

'Eastville recaptured its aura of the Fifties. It was a seething cauldron of football fanaticism which, from half-time onwards, must have created a nightmare atmosphere for Norwich's grossly overworked players.

'I cannot recall such a one sided encounter at Eastville as the second half and the period of extra time.'

Yet it was the visitors who took the lead, after 37 minutes: *'Trevor Howard hit a pass out to Self, on the right wing, who looked a good yard offside. Referee Mr Taylor looked to his linesman, who offered no signal. So the centre came in and Bennett steered it past Dick Sheppard.'*

Rovers didn't get back on level terms until the 64th minute: *'The ball came out to Jarman on the left, following a Ray Graydon free kick from the right. He pulled back a low pass for Stuart Taylor to at last beat Kevin Keelan with a finely controlled shot.'*

There were no further goals and so the tie went to extra time, with Rovers scoring twice just after the start of the second period: *'Within two minutes of the restart Megson, who had done so much to drive and direct Rovers' effort, hooked in a Stubbs pass to put his side ahead.*

'The joyous crescendo had scarcely had time to abate before Megson jumped for a Phil Roberts free kick, unsighting Keelan who allowed the ball to get past him for a third Rovers goal.

'Eastville's night to remember had reached a stunning climax.'

It's possible that the League Cup run affected Rovers' promotion challenge that season. There had been high hopes for Bill Dodgin's side following third-placed finish the previous year. However, they went on to finish sixth following their exploits in the competition, nine points adrift of runners-up Fulham and ten behind champions Preston.

Rovers: Sheppard, Roberts, Parsons, Prince, Taylor, Megson, Graydon, Jones (R), Stubbs, Jones (W), Jarman. Substitute: Gilbert.

Having beaten Second Division opposition in Norwich City in round three, Rovers faced another Second Division outfit, Birmingham City, in round four of the 1970/71 League Cup.

The game took place at Eastville on 27th October 1970 and Bill Dodgin's side ran out comfortable 3-0 winners.

Wayne Jones was left out of the starting line-up and Bobby Jones was injured, so Bryn Jones and Carl Gilbert came into the side.

The win was, apparently, every bit as decisive as the scoreline suggests: *'Bristol Rovers, a team containing six home-grown products, three free transfers, an exchange deal signing and a £10,000 buy, are in the quarter-finals of the League Cup.*

'In another Eastville night to remember, they earned a place among the last eight of the competition for the first time by sending Birmingham, one of the Second Division's more costly sides, the same way as Brighton, Newcastle and Norwich.'

Rovers took the lead after 14 minutes, with a somewhat fortuitous goal: *'There may have been a slice of luck about Rovers' first goal, which was turned into his own net off Roger Hynd's heels as Harold Jarman drove the ball across the goalmouth.'*

Our photo shows the ball entering the net while Jarman and Robin Stubbs are grounded, with Gilbert closing in.

'But the first half saw Dick Sheppard virtually untested while his opposite number, Mike Kelly, was the hero of one superlative save from Jarman and fine stops from Graydon and Gilbert.'

By all accounts, the second half was a one-sided affair and Rovers continued to take the game to their opponents: *'The outstanding Frankie Prince lashed a shot on to the post before Carl Gilbert celebrated his recall with a splendid goal.*

'It was the 65th minute when he met Jarman's free kick

from the left, hitting the ball left-footed on the run, volleying it savagely past Kelly.'

Birmingham's response was to take off 16-year-old Trevor Francis and bring on the experienced central defender John Sleeuwenhook, which allowed Hynd to push up in support of his forwards in an attempt to pull a goal back.

It was to no avail, though, and six minutes from time Rovers scored again: *'Jarman provided a perfect final pass from the left, in a move that cut through Birmingham's defence as if it wasn't there, for Stubbs to score with a perfectly controlled first-time shot.'*

Don Megson, Rovers player-coach made the following comment: *'People are asking me who I'd like in the next round. If we get another home draw, it doesn't matter who it is. With the Eastville roar behind us, we needn't be afraid of anyone.'*

Rovers: Sheppard, Roberts, Parsons, Prince, Taylor, Megson, Graydon, Gilbert, Stubbs, Jones (B), Jarman. Substitute: Jones (W).

League Cup Run Continues

Bradford Bashed!

Taken during the home game against Bradford City on 10th November 1970, this photo shows Harold Jarman, on the right, taking on three visiting defenders on a night when he scored a hat-trick in Rovers' 4-2 win.

Having registered a 4-0 win against Reading, also at Eastville, the previous Saturday, Rovers were set to name an unchanged side. But their visitors were struggling as several players had been hit by a gastric virus and a party of 16 set out from Bradford on Monday, to Ross-on-Wye, where they would stay before heading to Bristol on Tuesday evening.

Under the headline *'Fans go wild about Harold,'* the opening paragraph of the match report read as follows: *'They've renamed the Eastville North Stand Enclosure the Jarman Enclosure. And, last night, the fans who stand there went wild.'*

By all accounts, Rovers started the game well: *'The opening was breathtaking. Not many sides could have lived with Rovers in that mood. The pace and style of their attacking play was stunning.*

'It was Stuart Taylor who was first to score after four minutes, taking his goal well as Gilbert headed down a Graydon corner. But, even before that, Gilbert and Graydon (twice) had gone close.'

Jarman scored his first goal of the night with ten minutes on the clock: *"That gave me a lot of satisfaction. It's not often I*

head them in. Ray Graydon chipped up the centre and I timed my run in from the left just right."

Bruce Bannister, who was later to become a Rovers player, pulled a goal back for Bradford before half-time and Rovers fans had to wait until the 80th minute for their side's third goal.

It was the goal that Rovers needed and was smashed past goalkeeper Pat Liney by Jarman: *'It was a great move with Robin Stubbs, Ray Graydon and Carl Gilbert all doing well. The goalkeeper was very close when the ball got to me. I thought of trying to take it around him, but decided to hit it and it just squeezed past,'* said the goalscorer.

Jarman's first ever hat-trick for the club came four minutes later: *'It was a ball from Bryn Jones and ran perfectly for me to hit in.*

'I've waited for 12 years for that moment and I've never been so delighted in my life.

'I wasn't thinking in terms of a hat-trick after scoring the first two. But when the ball popped up in front of me, I thought this is it, this is the moment.

'I smashed it in and then ran to share the joy with the fans who always give me such great support.'

Rovers: Sheppard, Roberts, Parsons, Prince, Taylor, Megson, Graydon, Gilbert, Stubbs, Jones (B), Jarman. Substitute: Jones (R).

Third Division Rovers were beaten 3-1 by Fourth Division Aldershot in the second round of the 1969/70 FA Cup.

One year later, with the teams still in the same divisions, they met again at the same stage of the competition, and once again the game was to be played at Aldershot's Recreation Ground.

This photo comes from that game, played on 12th December 1970, when the sides drew 1-1 in front of a crowd of 7,748. Monday evening's report of the game read as follows: *'Dick Sheppard today revealed the story behind hi 60th-minute slip which cost Bristol Rovers victory at Aldershot in Saturday's FA Cup tie.*

'At 5am that morning, his wife Christine gave birth to a baby girl, the couple's second child, so Sheppard entered the match after a night of only two hours sleep.'

This is what the keeper had to say: *'Under the circumstances I didn't think I did too badly, but I should have held on to that shot. I went down too quickly to it. I thought the ball was coming faster than it actually was and virtually knocked it back to Dennis Brown.'*

As the report concluded, it was a gift that Brown could hardly refuse: *'The former Swindon forward gratefully chipped the ball back past Sheppard and into the net off the inside of the post, wiping out Harold Jarman's opener.'*

However Sheppard's error wasn't, the report said, the reason Rovers were unable to win the game: *'His mistake was the means by which Aldershot forced a replay. The fact that it was a goal the Fourth Division club so richly deserved was in no way the fault of the Rovers' goalkeeper.'*

In fact, Rovers had taken the lead after only eight minutes: *'Graydon seized on to a headed clearance out of Aldershot's defence, cutting in from the right before chipping over a centre.*

'Stubbs flicked the ball on to Jarman, who had moved in off the left wing. He met the ball in the centre of the goalmouth, heading it back inside the right-hand post.'

Overall, it doesn't appear to have been a particularly good game and became ill tempered before the final whistle, with Roberts being booked for a foul and Graydon for shouting at one of the linesmen: *'His uncharacteristic outburst was symptomatic of the frustration Rovers must have felt over their own inadequacy.'*

The result of the previous season could well have been repeated, as Walden and Brodie both hit the woodwork.

The replay took place at Eastville on 6th December and once again the Fourth Division outfit came out on top, winning 3-1 to progress the third round.

Rovers: Sheppard, Roberts, Parsons, Prince (Jones (W) 67), Taylor, Megson, Graydon, Gilbert, Stubbs, Jones (B), Jarman.

FA Cup Exit At The Hands Of Aldershot ... Again!

Fulham's Revenge

The home game against Fulham, on 13th February 1971, was the second of three meetings between the clubs in the 1970/71 campaign.

Rovers had already beaten the Cottagers 2-1 at Craven Cottage in the first round of that season's FA Cup, though the London outfit gained revenge in this fixture, winning 1-0 at Eastville in front of a crowd of 18,875.

It was Rovers' first home game for a month and the visitors arrived in Bristol a point behind second-placed Rovers

Kenny Stephens was recalled to the starting line-up in place of Ray Graydon who was left out because of illness, but Rovers were unable to register the win required to maintain their promotion push.

The opening paragraph of the match report sums up the afternoon for Bill Dodgin's side: *'Rovers paid a high price for missed chances at Eastville this afternoon where they lost their vital promotion clash with Fulham after attacking for most of the game.'*

The first half was goal-less, though Rovers created a number of scoring opportunities: *'Matthewson, lunging forward, managed to turn the ball behind with a brave header from Harold Jarman and a Carl Gilbert cross was deflected behind for a corner, while Wayne Jones fired wide.*

'Kenny Stephens should have put Rovers ahead when he eased past Callaghan, rounded Webster who had rushed off his line to the edge of the area, but shot wide.*

'Gilbert fired over the bar, and a Jarman header was scrambled away as Rovers continued to apply pressure on the visitors' defence.'

Dick Sheppard made a decent save from Steve Earle in the opening 45 minutes and denied the Fulham man again early in the second half before Rovers wasted an opportunity to take the lead: *'It was their best chance to date and came when Robin Stubbs was put clear by Gilbert, but shot wide when well placed.'*

It proved to be a costly miss as Fulham scored with 65 minutes on the clock: *'The scorer was Jimmy Conway, who was only just returned to the side after over three months on the injured list.*

'The ball came out to him on the right, from a scrambled clearance, and he beat Sheppard with a well directed cross-shot just inside the far post.

'As a result, Rovers lost their poise and control of midfield and might have conceded again, when Johnston shot straight at Sheppard.'

Our photo shows Harold Jarman going for goal.

Rovers: Sheppard, Roberts, Parsons, Prince, Taylor, Megson, Stephens, Stubbs, Gilbert (Jones (R), 75), Jones (W), Jarman.

On **13th March 1971, Rovers faced Tranmere Rovers at Eastville needing a win to maintain their hopes of gaining promotion to the Second Division.**

It didn't happen though, and the opening two paragraphs of the match report tell you why: *'The Eastville hoodoo struck again as Rovers crashed to their fourth successive home defeat, a result that virtually wrecked their promotion hopes.*

'Relegation-threatened Tranmere played an ultra defensive game in a bid to smother Rovers, and the plan worked almost to perfection.'

Striker Sandy Allan, whose goal the previous Tuesday had secured a 1-0 win at Doncaster, seemed the most likely Rovers player to get on the scoresheet: *'Three times in the opening 15 minutes he put the Merseysiders' defence under pressure, and was twice unlucky not to score.*

'The striker went close on a couple more occasions in the first half, but there were no goals.'

Five minutes into the second half, though, the visitors scored the only goal of the match: *'It was virtually Tranmere's first shot of the game and the only time Sheppard had done anything testing since the opening minute when he had stretched to gather Farrimond's free kick.*

'It was a breakaway goal, an attack through the middle leading to a rebound off Megson, running right for Crossley who took his chance well, beating Sheppard with a shot from the edge of the penalty area.'

The crowd of 9,249 weren't happy: *'The goal added to Rovers' disorder and to the discontent of their fans.*

'Tranmere defended in depth to preserve their lead, but almost snatched a second goal through Moore, who was denied by Sheppard.'

Our photo from the match shows Ray Graydon watching a Tranmere defender heading clear, while Harold Jarman is to the extreme right.

Defeat left Rovers in sixth place (that's where they ended the season) and Tranmere in 22nd, but they went on to avoid relegation finishing in 18th place. The relegated teams that season were Gillingham, Doncaster, Bury and Reading, while Fulham and Preston were promoted to the Second Division.

Rovers: Sheppard, Roberts, Parsons, Prince, Taylor, Megson, Graydon (Jones (R)), Jones (B), Stubbs, Allan, Jarman.

In the week leading up to the game, Alan Impey and Peter Aitken had been called up by Wales for a European youth tournament in Czechoslovakia in May, and striker Carl Gilbert had been sold to Rotherham for a fee of £10,000. General manager Bert Tann went on record as saying the money would be used to strengthen the squad in the summer.

We're Not Going Up!

Not A Good Easter!

On Tuesday 13th April 1971, Rovers played their third game of the Easter period when they entertained Plymouth Argyle at Eastville.

They had beaten Swansea 3-1 at the Vetch the previous Saturday, lost 2-0 at Chesterfield on Easter Monday and were beaten 3-1 by Plymouth in this game.

Our photo from that match shows Gordon Fearnley beating John Hore to the ball before getting in a cross. Sandy Allan is the Rovers player in the centre of the photo, while Harold Jarman is on the extreme right.

Rovers recalled Tom Stanton to the starting line-up, the first time he had been included in the first-team for 17 months. He replaced the injured Wayne Jones in midfield, and manager Bill Dodgin made three other changes.

Bryn Jones and Robin Stubbs were also carrying injuries, and were replaced by Bobby Brown and Fearnley respectively, while Kenny Stephens was dropped and Jarman recalled to the side.

The visitors had to endure an arduous journey to Bristol because of the holiday traffic: 'A police escort, a detour through country lanes and a sacrificed meal stop enabled Plymouth Argyle to reach Eastville just 31 minutes before kick off.

'By half time they must have been wondering whether the frantic dash had been worth all the effort.

'A goal down as a result of a refereeing decision that baffled everyone, all they had to be grateful for was that Rovers, and Ray Graydon in particular, were in such abysmal shooting form.

'Perhaps when they came out for the second half they had convinced themselves that things could only get better, and by 9.10pm all their earlier problems were forgotten.'

Although they dominated first-half proceedings, Rovers didn't take the lead until a minute before half-time: 'Furnell delayed making a clearance, standing just inside his penalty area and waving his team-mates upfield. Referee Dennis Turner awarded a free kick to Graydon, who was faced by a solid wall of Argyle defenders but somehow managed to squeeze a drive under the bar.'

Eight minutes into the second half, Plymouth equalised: 'It was a rare error by Frankie Prince, who failed to get away a hopeful cross into the middle by Davey, allowing Jimmy Hinch an unexpected chance he took well.'

Things got much worse for Rovers after that: 'Don Hutchens dashed across the face of the goal on to Keith Allen's free kick to hammer his side into a 78th minute lead, and four minutes from the end Davey, once a forward, forged his way up from the right-back position to whip a shot on the run past Sheppard.'

A crowd of 8,392 saw this Rovers side in action.

Rovers: Sheppard, Roberts, Parsons, Taylor, Stanton, Graydon, Brown, Allan, Fearnley, Jarman. Substitute: Jones (R).

Rovers faced Sunderland in the second round of the League Cup on 7th September 1971, just four days after thrashing Bradford City 7-1 in a Third Division match.

That game had seen veterans Harold Jarman and Bobby Jones score two goals apiece and Jarman was on target again in this match, against far more illustrious opposition.

Rovers were a goal ahead at the half-time interval: *'It was a great Jarman goal from Jones's centre that started the rot for Sunderland, and a Jarman pass that set up Wayne Jones to net the vital second just after half-time.*

'It was the penetrating running of 33-year-old Bobby Jones through the heart of Sunderland's massive defence that made Rovers such a menacingly effective attacking force.'

The Eastville visitors, apparently, had very little to offer: *'One lightning attack in the 16th minute, leading to a shot on to a post by little Bobby Kerr, proved what Sunderland could do if given the scope.*

'Rovers took note and there were only two other occasions in the game when Sunderland went anywhere near causing the Eastville side the same degree of danger.'

Both sides were awarded second-half penalties and the visitors managed to pull back a goal after Frankie Prince had tripped Dennis Tueart, thanks to the successful spot kick taken by Billy Hughes.

That came in the 64th minute of the game, and a minute later Kenny Stephens was fouled by Cec Irwin and Sandy Allan stepped up to dispatch the spot kick and give Rovers a 3-1 lead which they never looked in danger of surrendering.

There were no further goals and, as the visitors tired, the home side treated the crowd of 15,262.

'Rovers added that touch of panache they always seem to pull out on these occasions, making an effective performance an exciting one for the big crowd to watch.

'It took some great goalkeeping by Jim Montgomery to prevent Jarman and Jones scoring several more goals as the pair of them proved they have lost none of their great flair for the special occasion.

'But in Stephens they are gaining a rival crowd pleaser. The man who once quit soccer displayed a range of talent, delighting the fans with sprinting runs, delicate passes and clever floated shots.'

The Sunderland manager Alan Brown made just one post match comment, *"It was a very good game."*

Rovers skipper Brian Godfrey said: *"At times we played some great stuff. It was a tremendous team effort."*

Jarman is shown getting a shot away in our photo from the game.

Rovers: Sheppard, Roberts, Parsons, Godfrey, Taylor, Prince, Stephens, Jones (W), Allan, Jones (R), Jarman. Substitute: Stubbs.

Sunderland Sunk

A Costly Penalty Miss

The Third Division clash between Rovers and Aston Villa, on 2nd October 1971, drew a crowd of 20,428 to Eastville.

The majority of them, though, left disappointed as Villa secured a 1-0 win after Rovers had missed a penalty, taken by Sandy Allan and saved by Villa keeper Tommy Hughes.

Our photo from that game shows Harold Jarman in the centre, with Allan just in view over his shoulder, while Wayne Jones can be seen to the left of the photo. The Villa players are Keith Bradley, Ian 'Chico' Hamilton (in the background), Malcolm Beard and George Curtis.

Two players, Ray Graydon and Brian Godfrey, were facing their former clubs and it would appear that Godfrey gave the better performance on the day: *'Graydon was denied a goal on his return to Eastville by a superb reflex save by Dick Sheppard, and was robbed again by another fine save just before the end.*

'But, generally, he was kept subdued and it was Godfrey who impressed most of the two men facing their old team-mates.'

The first half was goal-less, with defences on top for most of the time, though Villa did go close to scoring when Sheppard touched a shot from Bruce Rioch over the bar and Andy Lochhead headed just wide before the keeper saved from Graydon.

Rovers were awarded a penalty two minutes into the second half: *'A long ball down Rovers left was nodded on by Allan for Jarman to chase and as the winger eased past Beard, he* was brought down just inside the penalty area.

'Both players were injured in the clash and it was another two minutes before the kick could be taken.

'Allan, successful with four out of four kicks so far this season, took the penalty and hit it well. But Hughes, diving low to his left, fisted the ball from inside the post and behind for a corner in a magnificent save.'

While Rovers apparently dominated possession after the spot kick, they conceded the game's only goal after 75 minutes: *'Villa took the lead against the run of play. Phil Roberts, injured in a tackle on the halfway line, had rolled off the field and Prince was also down hurt as Rioch pushed a pass into open space down the left.*

'Willie Anderson was on to it in a flash, cut inside the penalty area, and beat Sheppard with a well-placed shot tucked low down just inside the near post.'

Rovers: Sheppard, Roberts, Parsons, Godfrey, Taylor, Prince, Stephens (Green, 60), Jones (W), Allan, Jones (R), Jarman.

In the week leading up to the game, manager Bill Dodgin revealed that he was considering playing Jarman in home games only, and selecting Bryn Jones for away fixtures: *'We are moving more and more towards the squad system, where players are used for specific jobs. You make changes according to circumstances and who you are playing against, and the use of Harold for home games could come into this category.'*

It's hard to believe that it's almost forty years since Alan Warboys and Bruce Bannister – nicknamed 'Smash and Grab' – were terrorising Third Division defences.

Their popularity was such that a poster was produced, detailing the club's fixtures for 1973/74, billing them as the 'Deadliest Duo in the West.'

The photo reproduced here shows one of those posters displayed in what was the Bristol Omnibus Office in Bristol city centre. Whoever designed them knew what he or she was doing as the duo scored 40 goals between them that season, which saw Rovers finish second and gain promotion to Division Two.

Warboys contributed 22, Bannister 18 and the most famous victory of the campaign, an 8-2 win at Brighton, saw both grab a hat-tricks, though Warboys went one better than his strike partner and scored four goals against Brian Clough's team.

Bannister arrived at Eastville in November 1971 when Rovers paid Bradford City £23,000 to secure his services. A firm favourite with the fans, he went on to score 80 goals in 206 league games before a surprise move to Plymouth in December 1976. From Home Park, he moved to Hull City and enjoyed a spell in French football before retiring from the game.

Warboys signed for Rovers in March 1973. He had been an apprentice professional with Doncaster Rovers and made

40 appearances for them before joining Sheffield Wednesday. From Hillsborough he moved to Cardiff and then returned to Sheffield, signing for United. Rovers paid £35,000 to secure his services in March 1973 and he immediately forged a formidable strike partnership with Bannister on his arrival at Eastville.

After almost four years with the club and 53 goals in 144 appearances, he joined Fulham. From Craven Cottage he moved to Hull and in July 1979 he returned to his first club, Doncaster Rovers.

He played in a Rovers All Stars team prior to the Leyland Daf Final at Wembley in 1990, and on a visit to the Memorial Stadium a few years back, he recalled his fond memories of the club and was visibly moved when everyone in the bar gave him a rousing send off with their version of 'Goodnight Irene.'

I'm not sure how many posters were printed, but it would be interesting to know if any Rovers supporters have held on to one, as it constitutes a unique piece of Rovers memorabilia.

Smash and Grab

Reserves At Eastville

This photo was taken during the reserve team game against West Ham at Eastville on 16th February 1974.

Central defender Graham Day appears to have won this aerial challenge against two West Ham players, while striker Wayne Powell looks on.

The Hammers won the game 1-0 and the brief match report ran as follows: *'Failure to turn the chances they created in to goals proved costly for Rovers as they tamely surrendered both points in this Football Combination fixture.*

'Rovers badly missed the finishing of David John, who was surprisingly relegated to the substitutes bench.

'John made a belated appearance in the 77th minute when he replaced centre-forward Powell. West Ham's goal was scored by Yilmes Orhan in the 73rd minute.'

Graham Day, now mine host at the Flowerpot Inn, Kingswood, represented Bristol Boys from U-11 through to the U-15s and was playing for Bristol City's 'A' side at the age of 15. The expected offer of an apprenticeship never materialised though and he signed for Bristol St George.

It was Joe Davis, a former Rovers player, who recommended Graham to try his luck at Eastville and, after graduating through the 'A' team and reserves he eventually made his first-team debut, against Fulham, in March 1975.

From then until 1979 he was a regular in the first-team, partnering Stuart Taylor at the heart of the defence.

Despite being in a struggling Rovers side, he also played alongside some of the world's greatest players of the time thanks to three spells with Portland Timbers in America.

Twice he joined the Timbers on loan before finally making the move permanent when former Rovers boss Don Megson paid £40,000 to secure his signature.

During his time in America he rubbed shoulders with the likes of Pele, Alberto, Best, Cruyff, Muller and Beckenbauer.

However it all came to an end with the collapse of the National League and on his return to this country, he signed for Forest Green Rovers and appeared for them in the FA Vase Final at Wembley.

He did enjoy a short spell with Bournemouth at the same time as Best, but his only appearance for them was in a Hampshire Cup final.

He ended his career at Bath City, where he picked up a Somerset Cup medal to go with the one he gained from his appearance in the Hampshire Final and the Gloucester Cup medal he picked up when with Rovers – quite a unique hat-trick!

The team that faced West Ham in the reserve team match back in 1974 was as follows:

Crabtree, Bater, Moore, Day, Aitken, Coombes, Britton, Jones, Powell, (John (D), John (M), Williams (G).

On **2nd March 1974 Rovers slipped to a third successive away defeat at Home Park Plymouth.**

It was a severe blow to their hopes of winning the Third Division title that season, but the way they played on a mudbath of a pitch impressed Plymouth boss Tony Waiters.

'Rovers will go up. There is no doubt in my mind about that. It is just a question of which promotion place they will fill,' he said.

'I have a lot of admiration for them. They don't know what it is to pack in a fight. There is a real character in the side and that is why I was delighted with my team's part in this game.'

The only goal of the game came nine minutes into the second half.

Stephen Davy met Hughie Reed's inswinging corner from the left, his flicked header dropped and stuck in the mud giving Davie Provan a chance to score from close range.

Rovers were without first team regulars Alan Warboys, Colin Dobson, John Rudge and Frankie Prince for this game, while manager Don Megson said that conditions were so bad that it was obvious it was going to be a game won or lost on a mistake or the run of the ball.

This photo, taken at that game, shows Kenny Stephens taking on two Argyle defenders.

Stephens, who was born in Bristol, began his footballing career with West Bromwich Albion after joining as an apprentice professional in 1962.

He went on to make 22 league appearances for the Baggies before moving to Walsall in December 1968.

However his career with the Saddlers was short-lived and after only seven league appearances he announced his retirement from the game at the age of 21.

He became a newsagent in the Midlands but was persuaded to come out of retirement by his former Albion team-mate and fellow Bristolian Dick Sheppard, who had returned to his home city to play for Rovers.

Stephens eventually completed his move to Eastville in October 1970 and went on to score 11 goals in 225 league appearances in his seven years with Rovers.

He ended his career with Hereford, making 60 league appearances for the Edgar Street outfit.

In front of a Home Park crowd of 11,374 Rovers lined up as follows: Eadie, Jacobs, Green, Taylor, Parsons, Prince (Aitken), Stephens, Stanton, Fearnley, Bannister, Jones.

Defeat At Plymouth

Three Wise Men!

This is a photo that will stir the memories of Rovers supporters old enough to recall the 1974 promotion season, when the team finished in second place in the old Third Division, just a point behind champions Oldham Athletic.

Mike Green, Frankie Prince and Colin Dobson stand together, hands on hips, as though they can't believe what's just happened.

Rovers have just lost their first home game of the 1973/74 campaign, 2-0 at the hands of Walsall, in front of an Eastville crowd of 11,370 on 23rd March 1974.

Mike Green was Rovers' captain that season, having been signed from Gillingham in July 1971. He scored twice in 75 league appearances for Rovers but was, surprisingly, released by the club before the start of the new Second Division campaign. He remained in the Third Division following his move to Plymouth for a fee of £19,000, and he skippered them to promotion in his first season at Home Park.

He moved to Torquay in March 1977 and was player-manager at Plainmoor from March 1977 to May 1981.

Frankie Prince was a graduate of Rovers' South Wales nursery who went on to make 362 league appearances for the club during almost 13 years at Eastville. A tough-tackling midfielder, he was a member of the Watney Cup-winning side of 1972 and missed only three games of the 1973/74 promotion campaign. He won four Welsh U-23 caps and although he was a substitute for a full international against England in 1972, he never got off the bench.

On leaving Rovers, he moved to Exeter but played in just 27 league games for them. He undertook a variety of jobs outside of the game until returning to professional football as community officer for Torquay United in 1992, a position he still holds.

Having started his career with Sheffield Wednesday, where he won two England U-23 caps, Colin Dobson moved to Huddersfield in 1966 after 177 league games for the Owls.

Another 149 league games for the Terriers followed and he spent six months on loan at Brighton before joining Rovers as player-coach in June 1972.

Just as Green and Prince were important members of the 1973/74 promotion side, Dobson's experience was invaluable. He made 39 appearances during that season and registered the 100th goal of his career against Tranmere, quite a milestone for a left-winger.

He remained in the game after leaving the club, working for Coventry City, Port Vale and Aston Villa as a coach, as well as coaching in the United Arab Emirates.

They might have won promotion to the Second Division at the end of the 1973/74 season, but Rovers failed to make an impact on the pop charts of the time!

Pictured here in London's Carnaby Street are five members of the squad who had all travelled up to the capital to record a song with Rod Hull and Emu!

I wonder how many supporters reading this have a copy of 'Bristol Rovers – All The Way' and will actually own up to it? Sung to the tune of 'She'll Be Coming Round The Mountain' the record failed to make the charts – I wonder why!

The guy on the left of the photo was friends with a number of the players, though his name escapes me! Next to him stand Kenny Stephens, Dave Staniforth, Lindsay Parsons, Trevor Jacobs and Dick Sheppard.

Although born in Bristol, Stephens had joined West Brom as an apprentice professional in 1962 and later signed for Walsall. He joined Rovers in 1970 and made 31 appearances in the promotion-winning side.

Staniforth was a relative newcomer to the club, having signed from Sheffield United in March 1974. He did make 11 appearances before the end of that successful season, and remained at Eastville until the end of the 1978/79 season when he joined Bradford City. By that time he had registered 32 goals in 151 appearances for the club.

Parsons, born in Barton Hill, had already spent 13 years with the club as an apprentice and a pro when promotion was achieved. The reliable left-back missed just four games that season and remained at Eastville until July 1977, when he joined Torquay.

Jacobs, another Bristolian, made his name during 131 appearances for Bristol City prior to his release at the end of the 1972/73 season. The right-back quickly adapted to life with the blue half of Bristol and was an ever-present in the side that clinched promotion to the Second Division. He left the club in 1977, having made 83 appearances.

Like Stephens, goalkeeper Sheppard was a Bristolian who made his pro debut in the colours of West Brom, where he had been an apprentice from 1960. He joined Rovers on a free transfer in 1969 and his penalty save in the 1972 Watney Cup Final earned Rovers the trophy. Sadly, his career was brought to a premature end when he suffered a depressed fracture of the skull in a match against Chesterfield in January 1973. He didn't make any appearances during the promotion season and although he played one game in the following campaign and two more for Torquay during a loan spell at Plainmoor, they were the last games of his league career.

Carnaby Street

Wayne's World

A **match against Ipswich Town on Tuesday 3rd September 1974 brought the curtain down on a year of testimonial events for Wayne Jones.**

This photo was taken at one of a number of pubs visited for a skittles or darts evening during that time. *'We seemed to attend many similar functions during Wayne's testimonial year,'* recalled his former team-mate Peter Aitken. *'There would be a darts or skittles match taking place and we ended with a raffle. All the proceeds from the evenings went towards Wayne's testimonial fund and there was a great deal of interest in the evenings because the whole squad would almost always be in attendance and, of course, it was a promotion season.'*

Jones had been injured in a match against Brentford in November 1972. It was thought that he had torn a cartilage, but it turned out that he had an arthiritic knee condition and his playing career was over.

At the age of 24, he had already made 224 league appearances for the club after signing pro forms in 1966. His form had earned him six Welsh U-23 caps and he had won his first full cap playing for his country against Finland in May 1971.

Whilst I can name the players in the photo above, I'm not certain which pub it's taken in, neither do I know the identity of the gentlemen holding the football with Wayne, or the one to his left.

As for the others, Bobby Jones, who had retired in 1973,

is on the extreme left of the photo and is the only squad member wearing a tie. Next to him is goalkeeper Paul Lewis, and then comes the familiar face of Peter Aitken, who appeared in 234 league games for the club and is now our Football in the Community Officer. (He had rather more hair in those days!)

According to Peter, the players next to him are youngsters Ray Williams and Jon Moore, whilst standing in front of them, next to Wayne, is another goalkeeper, Richard Crabtree. Record appearance holder Stuart Taylor is next in line. He ended his Rovers career with 546 league games to his name and he's stood next to another central defender, Graham Day.

Stood between Stuart and Graham is Trevor Jacobs, who had joined Rovers from Bristol City in the summer of 1973, and the line-up is completed by Gordon Fearnley and Frankie Prince. Fearnley also played football in America on leaving Eastville, and he stayed in the States after qualifying as an American lawyer.

Frankie, meanwhile, remained involved in the game and in July 2012 completed 20 years service as Torquay's Football in the Community Officer.

Wayne, who qualified as a physiotherapist following his injury, has also stayed in the game and has served a number of clubs in his time, including Gillingham, Hereford and Yeovil. In the summer of 2012 he was with Newport County.

I suspect that this photo of Eastville was taken in the mid-1970s.

The elevated section of the M32 can be seen in the background, but the famous flowerbeds, situated behind each goal, were still there and those in front of the Tote End are clearly visible.

The stadium was originally home to Bristol Harlequins Rugby Club, but was purchased by the directors of Eastville Rovers in 1896. The club developed a stadium with a capacity of 20,000 and, on 5th April 1897, played their first game there. The match, against Aston Villa, ended in a 5-0 defeat.

The South Stand, on the right of the photo, was completed in 1924 whilst the open terrace at the far end of the ground, the Muller Road End, was constructed in 1931.

There were ambitious plans to provide a roof for all who stood there but the board of directors, after considering plans put forward by Messrs Maynard, Froude and Stevens, decided that it would be too costly.

The North Stand, which is situated to the left of the photo and not in shot, was built in 1958, whilst the Tote End, from where the photo was taken, was built in 1935 and modernised in 1961. Floodlights were installed in 1959 and the first game under lights took place in September of that year.

In the early part of the twentieth century, the ground was used for a number of community as well as sporting events. Charity carnivals were regularly held there, whilst in the 1930s the ground was used as a venue for professional athletics meetings.

American servicemen stationed in the area played American Football at Eastville between 1944 and 1948 and for a number of years the ground hosted an annual firework display, organised by the Bristol Evening Post.

The car park hosted funfairs and circuses and became home to a regular Sunday market in 1967 and a Friday market in 1972.

The Harlem Globetrotters played an exhibition match at the stadium, speedway attracted large crowds for two seasons in the mid-1970s, Gloucestershire Cricket Club staged a benefit match for Zaheer Abbas in 1984 and there was a brief return of American Football in 1986.

However, the arrival of greyhound racing, in 1932 signalled the end of the club's ownership of its own ground.

In 1939 the club was £16,000 in debt and chairman Fred Ashmead agreed to sell the venue to the Greyhound Company as Rovers became tenants at the ground. It was a situation that continued beyond the fire which destroyed the South Stand in 1980, until the club moved into exile, in Bath, in 1986.

Eastville – Rovers' Spiritual Home

Defeat At The Valley

Prior to travelling to London for this game on 17th January 1976, Rovers announced that they hoped to take in a three-game tour of Turkey.

It was suggested that the games would be against Galatasaray, Besiktas and Altay.

The Saturday following the Charlton match was FA Cup day and Rovers had bowed out of the competition at the third round stage, when they were beaten by Chelsea. This meant that there would be time to fit in an overseas trip before their next league fixture.

By the time they set off for Charlton, tour details had been agreed in principle and just required the sanction of the two national Football Associations. There was, though, a hitch over the payment of the air fares as the Telex lines were down.

The game at The Valley virtually ended any hopes that Rovers might have had of being involved in the Second Division promotion race, as they went down 3-0. However, Don Megson's side appear to have played well and all three Charlton goals were described as a joke by the manager.

The first arrived after only two minutes: *'Jim Eadie seemed so long dropping the ball it just wasn't true. He seemed to have Mark Randall's low, long-range shot well covered then, all of a sudden, the ball was popping about and George Hope couldn't fail to score.'*

A second goal was conceded on 33 minutes. *'The keeper's reactions were not what they should have been when Keith Peacock hit a shot on to the bar and Derek Hales followed up to make it 2-0.'*

Two minutes from time the home side scored again: *'Graham Day, who had his worst game ever in a Rovers shirt, was caught on the wrong side of Hales when the man of the match added Charlton's third goal before the end.'*

As for Rovers, the report concluded that they had been unlucky to lose so heavily: *'After conceding the early goal, only two fine saves from Graham Tutt denied goals for Bruce Bannister and Alan Warboys.*

'It was unfortunate that Warboys didn't reappear for the second half, due to a gashed ankle, but substitute Wayne Powell went close when he headed against the bar and the rebound fell to a home defender.'

This first-half photo shows Charlton keeper Tutt under pressure from Warboys while Bannister (No 10) looks on.

Rovers lined up as follows in front of a crowd of 8,598: Eadie, Bater, Day, Taylor, Parsons, Aitken, Stephens, Williams, Dobson, Warboys (Powell), Bannister.

As for the tour to Turkey, it never happened.

Manager Megson said: *"The original Turkish offer guaranteed all our expenses and allowed for the possibility of a profit. Later messages changed those terms, so we called the trip off."*

Southampton arrived at Eastville on 17th April 1976 as FA Cup finalists having beaten Crystal Palace 2-0 in the semi-final.

They also harboured ambitions of achieving promotion to the First Division, but defeat against Rovers that afternoon was to end their slim chances.

Rovers ran out 2-0 winners courtesy of two goals from Frankie Prince, their first home win since 31st January.

The game was played just 24 hours after Rovers had fought out a Good Friday goal-less draw with local rivals Bristol City in front of a crowd of 26,430. Two days after the game against Southampton, Don Megson's team travelled to Kenilworth Road to take on Luton Town. Very little rest and no iced baths to aid recovery back then!

The first goal arrived after only four minutes: *'Prince headed home from a centre by right-winger Martyn Britten, who ran on to a crossfield pass from Lindsay Parsons, recalled to left-back.'*

Prince was on target again thirty minutes later: *'His second goal came from the penalty spot after an award by referee Bert Newsome which left Southampton manager Lawrie McMenemy and his players speechless. The only exception was Hugh Fraser, who argued and had his name taken.*

'Southampton had some cause for complaint. Prince undoubtedly fouled goalkeeper Ian Turner but, with Turner in possession of the ball, referee Newsome ignored the incident.

'Turner retaliated, however, with his elbow and that led to the penalty which saw Prince drive the ball home from the spot.'

Southampton seldom showed as an attacking force in that first half, apart from a header by Peter Osgood and a shot from Mick Channon.

It was much the same story after the break, though an Osgood header saw Jim Eadie make a fine save and the keeper was quickly off his line to deny Channon a shooting opportunity, while Pat Earles glanced a header wide late in the game.

As it was, there were no further goals and Rovers held out to record the win that saw them mathematically safe from relegation.

Southampton boss McMenemy was far from pleased with his side's performance, saying: *'The first half was a shambles and those players wanting to go to Wembley will have to play to earn a place in our remaining league fixtures.'*

Nevertheless, eight of the team that faced Rovers were in the side that beat Manchester United in the FA Cup final on 1st May.

Our photo shows Kenny Stephens closing down Peter Osgood during the game, which was watched by a crowd of 11,834.

Rovers: Eadie, Williams, Parsons, Day, Taylor, Prince, Britten, Smith, Staniforth, Bater (Stephens, 64), Evans.

Southampton Scuppered

A Welcome Win

n 11th September 1976, Orient arrived at Eastville having picked up their first point of the season in a 2-2 draw against Plymouth the previous week.

Rovers, on the other hand, had lost to a George Best inspired Fulham in their previous game and reports revealed that manager Don Megson had his players concentrating on passing in training in the build-up to this game. Phil Bater and Dave Staniforth had been injured in the single goal defeat at Craven Cottage, but had recovered to take their place in the squad.

Our photo shows Alan Warboys scoring the only goal of the game, which came in the 38th minute. However the headline above the match report (*'Rovers turn fans jeers to cheers'*) indicated that it wasn't a game for the purist: *'Even their faithful 5,000 fans turned on Bristol Rovers at Eastville on Saturday.*

'But the players response to being slo-handclapped by their most loyal supporters delighted Don Megson and resulted in a desperately needed first home win of the season.'

Indeed, the fans weren't happy with the first thirty minutes of the match, when a *'punchless Orient were content to stop Rovers playing.'* Rovers gradually upped the tempo, though: *'Towards half-time Warboys and Kenny Stephens began to make an impact on the game. Appropriately, they were the players who combined to produce a goal of sufficient quality to compensate for the dreary opening.'*

Megson gave particular praise to the part Bater played in clipping a quick free kick wide to Stephens, instead of swinging the ball directly into the goalmouth: *'It caught Orient's defence off guard and Warboys scored with a textbook far-post header.'*

As for Orient, they seldom threatened a goal before the break and only really had two clear chances in the second half, both from free kicks taken by central defender Phil Hoadley, the second of which produced a fine save from Jim Eadie.

Manager Megson had this to say after the match: *'We were producing rubbish and the crowd had every right to slow handclap. It seemed to trigger off something in the lads and all of a sudden they started to give the fans something to cheer about, and cheer they did.'*

The report was critical of the performance of some of the Rovers players: *'Martyn Britten's return to the left-wing was disappointing and, again, Wilf Smith didn't look the answer to Rovers' midfield problem and looked happier late in the game when he reverted to his normal full-back position after Bater had gone off with a recurrence of thigh trouble.'*

A crowd of 5,493 saw this Rovers side in action: Eadie, Aitken, Bater (Staniforth, 74), Day, Taylor, Prince, Stephens, Smith, Warboys, Bannister, Britten.

This photo shows Dave Staniforth scoring Rovers' winner in the 2-1 win against Carlisle at Eastville on 12th December 1976.

While a number of games across the country were called off because of frozen conditions, the Eastville pitch was declared playable – though Rovers boss Don Megson wasn't best pleased: *'I like games that are decided by footballing strengths and weaknesses and not by whether a player slips at a vital moment because of a treacherous pitch,'* he said.

Reports suggest that Carlisle, with the experienced Bobby Moncur controlling things from the back, adapted to the difficult conditions better than Rovers: *'They kept a better footing and were more accurate with their passing.'*

The two goalkeepers on view had contrasting games: *'Rovers could argue that they were foiled three times only by the brilliance of Carlisle goalkeeper Martin Burleigh, who pulled off tremendous saves from Dave Staniforth in the first half, and David Williams and Gordon Fearnley in the second.*

'But again Jim Eadie in Rovers goal, was not impressive. The Scotsman was at fault when Carlisle took the lead with Billy Rafferty's 11th goal of the season, tamely palming down a Mike Barry free kick to the former Plymouth striker's feet.'

That goal came on 24 minutes, but Rovers were back on level terms 12 minutes later: *'Gordon Fearnley showed cool opportunism when firing home a first-time shot for his fifth goal of the season.'*

The winning goal came nine minutes from time: *'Dave Staniforth flicked a precise header past the splendid Burleigh from a Fearnley cross.'*

Two Rovers players made the headlines after the game when it was revealed that one would be staying, while the other was almost certain to move on.

Fearnley was the man to remain at Eastville: *'Transfer-listed at the end of last season, Fearnley is no longer up for sale and is now firmly established in his true role of striker for the first time since joining Rovers from Sheffield Wednesday six years ago.'*

The player on the move was Bruce Bannister, and this was to be his last game in Rovers colours and he joined Plymouth Argyle four days later: *'It didn't really matter that Bannister, the buoyant striker who thrives on goals, failed to score on his farewell performance at frost-bound Eastville.*

'As the meagre crowd made for the exits, some 500 young supporters waited behind to voice noisy approval of Bannister's services.

'Yet Bannister, never a man to shun the spotlight, failed to show up and the fans dispersed.'

'I wanted to go out to see them,' he said afterwards, *'but the boss wouldn't let me, so I stayed inside.'*

A crowd of 5,496 saw this Rovers team in action: Eadie, Bater, Parsons, Prince, Taylor, Williams, Stephens, Fearnley, Warboys, Bannister, Staniforth. Substitute: Evans.

Bruce Bows Out

The Don Of Eastville

Pictured in the dugout is Don Megson, Bristol Rovers manager between July 1972 and November 1977.

Prior to his move to Eastville as player-coach in March 1970, Megson had spent his entire playing career with Sheffield Wednesday, appearing in 386 league games for the Owls.

He also captained Wednesday in the 1966 FA Cup final and represented the Football League against their Italian counterparts in November 1960.

He made his Rovers league debut in a 1-0 home win against Leyton Orient in March, though it soon became apparent that manager Bill Dodgin had brought Megson to the club not only to sustain a promotion push, but to groom him as his successor.

The promotion bid ended in failure as Rovers finished in third place behind Luton and Orient, but hopes were high for a successful campaign in 1970/71. Megson featured in 24 league games that season, but once again Rovers missed out on promotion and finished in sixth place.

By the start of the 1971/72 season, Megson had stepped down as a player to concentrate on his coaching duties. Once again, Rovers finished in sixth place and at the end of that season, Dodgin reverted to the post of chief scout, allowing Megson to take over as manager.

His first games in charge were in the Watney Cup, a competition for the league's highest-scoring non-promoted teams from the previous season. Rovers won a dramatic penalty shoot-out to win the final against Sheffield United at Eastville to get his managerial career off to a sensational start.

In the league, he led the club to fifth place and in 1973/74 succeeded in leading them out of the Third Division. They should have ended the campaign as champions, having been undefeated in their first 27 league games. At one stage they were seven points clear at the top of the table, but gradually that lead was whittled away and in the end they had to settle for runners-up spot behind Oldham Athletic.

Although he managed to keep the club in the Second Division, a lack of finance hampered progress and they were always struggling to stay free of the relegation positions.

In November 1977, he accepted a three-year contract to manage Portland Timbers in the North American League. Citing the lack of finance as one of his reasons for leaving, said: *'It brought frustration for the club, for the supporters and for me and it came to the point where I felt it was probably in everyone's interests that there should be a change.'*

On 14th January 1978, Rovers travelled to Craven Cottage for a Second Division fixture against Fulham and came away with a hard-earned point from a 1-1 draw.

Over 700 Rovers fans made their way to the capital on a charter train, the first football special to be organised by Rovers Away Travel Service (RATS).

Outlining the new travel scheme in the matchday programme for the game against Sunderland in December 1977, commercial manager Graham Drew advised fans that: *'It costs £1 to join and members will be issued with an identity card with their picture on it. On production of this, the holder will be entitled to a 10% discount off the price of official travel organised by Rovers Supporters Club.*

'Probably the best way to join is to come on the RATS special train to Fulham on 14th January. The cost of £4.50 will cover the day's return fare, enrol you as a member of RATS and also give you the Service's special Rovers scarf.

'The team will also be travelling on that train to London, along with the Presidents Club. There will be catering facilities provided on the train.'

A Paul Randall goal, one of 20 he scored that season, earned the point in front of a crowd of 8,424 and Rovers lined up as follows:

Thomas, Aitken, Bater, Harding, Taylor (S), Prince, Barry, Pulis, Gould, Staniforth, Randall.

The photo reproduced here shows some of the fans on the return journey, accompanied by Mike Barry (with the nice perm!), and manager Bobby Campbell.

Graham Drew is pictured on the extreme left, in the sheepskin jacket, while Sandra Jacques, who still sells 50/50 tickets on matchdays, is stood next to the manager.

You may also recognise a very young Steve Burns on the right of the photo, in a very stylish 'cardy', though it's a good job that it's a black and white photo, as a colour one would undoubtedly damage the eyesight!

In his programme article following that trip, Drew said: *'The venture went so well that another train has been organised for the next away match at Luton. Everyone who went on the first trip automatically became members of RATS.*

'I would like to congratulate the fans on their exemplary behaviour and the wonderful support they gave the team, which was so much appreciated by the players and the manager.

'It was a nice final touch when Bobby Campbell and the players walked the length of the train on the return journey to chat to the supporters and thank them for their support.'

Rovers fielded the same starting eleven against Luton, a game which also finished 1-1 with Steve Harding scoring the goal that earned Campbell's side a share of the spoils.

RATS

Staniforth Scores

Taken at Eastville on 25th November 1978, this photo shows Dave Staniforth in action against Sheffield United, his former club.

It was quite a special afternoon as Rovers won 2-0 and Staniforth, who was captain of the Rovers side, scored one of the goals.

In addition, there were presentations before the match, to manager Bobby Campbell and central defender Stuart Taylor.

'Rovers manager Bobby Campbell received a gallon of whisky and Stuart Taylor a magnum of champagne on celebrations day at Eastville, but skipper Dave Staniforth reckoned his present was best in the 2-1 victory over Sheffield United.'

The presentation to Campbell was to mark his first anniversary as manager after succeeding Don Megson, whilst the game marked Taylor's 500th league appearance for the club.

'Staniforth's superbly-headed early goal from Mike Barry's corner helped Rovers on their way to yet another home win. Steve Finnieston equalised on 62 minutes, but Paul Randall nodded in the winner five minutes later on to register his 13th goal of the season.'

"It's always good to score against your old club, but this one was particularly satisfying," was Staniforth's post-match comment.

A crowd of 8,434 saw Rovers line up as follows: Thomas, Aitken, Bater (White), Day, Taylor, Hendrie, Dennehy, Williams, Staniforth, Randall, Barry.

Born in Chesterfield, Staniforth joined Sheffield United as an apprentice after leaving school and was awarded his first pro contract as a 17-year-old. In only his second league game for the Blades, he scored twice in a 3-0 win against Blackburn Rovers.

He played 26 league games for United before moving to Eastville in March 1974. Writing in the matchday programme a few weeks before his first game as skipper, ironically against his former club at Bramall Lane, he had this to say: *'Paul Randall and I seem to have got a good working relationship going. I'm quite useful in the air and try to get as many flick-ons as possible so that Paul can use his pace to take the ball on through defences.'*

'The system worked particularly well when we had Bobby Gould out on the right-wing, hitting early balls into me. Now Bobby has moved on to Hereford United and Mike Barry is producing a similar service from the other flank. And we are working on getting Miah Dennehy to take the ball to the bye-line and cut it back so that we get a variety of service.'

He scored 32 goals in 151 league games for Rovers and, on leaving the club, moved back to Yorkshire where he completed over 100 league games for Bradford City before

This photo shows manager Bobby Campbell standing in the Eastville dugout (to the left of the tunnel as we look at it).

I can only assume that it was taken during his reign as manager between November 1977 and December 1979.

Born in Glasgow in 1922, Campbell began his distinguished footballing career with Scottish junior outfit Glasgow Perthshire and was given the chance to sign for Falkirk. However, World War Two meant it was an offer he had to refuse and, like so many footballers of his generation, his career was put on hold until the end of hostilities.

Not that the war stopped him playing, as he represented the Army and Armed Services representative side.

He did sign for Falkirk once the war was over and, in May 1947, he joined Chelsea for a fee of £12,000. That same month, he won the first of five full Scottish international caps when he turned out for his country against Belgium.

He went on to score 36 goals in his 188 league appearances for Chelsea before moving to Reading in August 1954. His playing career came to an end three years later, but he remained on the staff at Reading until 1961 when he became manager of Dumbarton.

One year later, he arrived at Eastville as trainer/coach, beginning an 18-year association as an employee of the club, though his affection for Rovers remained and he attended games at the Memorial Stadium until shortly before his death in 2009.

Many young players at the club at that time were given their taste of first-team football by Campbell, including Martin Thomas, Steve White, Paul Randall and Gary Mabbutt, all of whom were transferred for large fees.

As far as this photo is concerned, I have no idea who Rovers were playing as I don't recognise the opposition manager in the other dugout.

Standing between the dugouts though, behind the policeman, are Andrew Evans and Geraint Williams. Those two certainly had contrasting careers. Evans was forced to retire from the game after sustaining an injury against Southampton in October 1977. Although he remained at the club and began taking his qualifications in coaching and treatment of injuries, he eventually decided to make a clean break from football.

Williams, on the other hand, moved on to Derby County and then Ipswich before becoming a manger, firstly with Colchester United and, more recently, Leyton Orient.

Campbell In The Dugout

Pirates Beat Pensioners!

Wouldn't it be nice to think that Rovers could beat Chelsea 3-0 again in the not too distant future?

However, it's unlikely to happen whilst the London outfit continue to be bankrolled by Roman Abramovich. The gulf between the two sides at the moment is huge, yet back in 1979/80 they were both in the Second Division.

The photo shows Shaun Penny celebrating one of his two goals that afternoon. He is being congratulated by David Williams whilst in the background Gary Mabbutt, right arm raised, salutes the goal.

'Penny's first goal, on 27 minutes, was driven in from close range after a cross-shot from the vastly improved Vaughan Jones rebounded from the top of Chelsea's near post.

'The second was run in as Tony Pulis chipped a shot over the advancing Iles and was followed, a minute later, by a marvellous first-time drive by Pulis which finally killed off Chelsea's hopes.'

The future Rovers manager Bobby Gould was assistant manager at Stamford Bridge at the time and he had this to say afterwards: *'Rovers' recent record speaks for itself and we have had them looked at. Harold Jarman is doing a tremendous job. His management and Terry Cooper's contribution on the field seem a*

perfect combination. The way Terry uses his experience is something you can't buy, however much money you have to spend.'

At a time when two points were awarded for a win, this was Rovers twelfth point from their last nine games, a run of results which, ultimately, staved off the threat of relegation.

They finished the season in 19th place with 35 points, 13 more than bottom club Charlton who were relegated to the Third Division along with Burnley and Fulham. Our visitors that afternoon would come to regret dropping two points as they finished in fourth place on 53 points. That was the same number as third-placed Birmingham, one fewer than second-placed Sunderland and two less than champions Leicester.

The game, watched by a crowd of 14,176, was marred by the behaviour of some fans in the Chelsea end, who knocked down a wall supporting the Muller Road terraces.

Rovers: Thomas, Jones, Cooper, Aitken, Taylor, Prince (Emmanuel), Barrowclough, Williams, Penny, Mabbutt, Pulis.

As well as Gould, there was another future Rovers boss on view that day. Dennis Rofe was in the Chelsea side. He took over the managerial reins during our exile at Twerton Park and was in charge from October 1991 to November 1992.

Taken on 15th March 1980, this photo shows Keith Brown in action for the reserves against Oxford, a game which ended in a 0-0 draw.

Brown joined Rovers in 1977 from Bristol St George and made his first-team debut when going on as a substitute against Brighton in April 1979. He made another substitute appearance in May against Cardiff and was in the starting line-up for the final league match of the 1978/79 season against Wrexham.

He made three more league appearances the following season and another against Notts County in 1980/81.

He joined Bath City at the end of that season and moved on to Cheltenham in 1986, only to return to Twerton Park in 1988. In all, he made 372 appearances for Bath and was rewarded for his service to them with a testimonial match against Crystal Palace.

He was always on the fringe of the first-team during his time at Eastville, but was top scorer for the reserves in 1979/80.

He was 18 when signed by Rovers and a mechanical engineer by trade. At the time this photo was taken, he was still hopeful of playing regularly in Rovers' first-team. Writing in the match programme in April 1980, he said: *'Not serving a soccer apprenticeship, I have needed to catch up on lost time and believe I have made progress this season.*

'I know I must improve on my heading and put more aggression into my game. My speed over 10 or 15 yards is my main strength and it is a matter of me putting it to the best use.

'I am beginning to get the feel of league football but must admit that I am still a bit nervous and need some help and direction on the field.

'Rovers offered me a trial after I played against their youth side for Bristol St George's U-18 team. A month later, I was given the chance to sign as a full professional and I jumped at it.

'That meant giving up an engineering apprenticeship but it wasn't a difficult decision, because all my life I have only ever really wanted to be a footballer.

'But I am still attending college each week to continue my engineering studies. If things don't work out for me in league football, I will need to have something to fall back on.'

He revealed that he had played for Bristol Boys from U-11 through to U-15 before joining Bristol St George, and that he had also played a couple of games for Minehead prior to his move to Rovers, but that his heart was now set on a career in the pro game: *'My priority is to establish myself in the first team at Eastville.'* Although he never quite achieved success with Rovers, he enjoyed a long and successful career in non-league football.

In November 2009 he was in charge of Shepton Mallet when Rovers sent a side down to Somerset to celebrate the turning on of the club's new floodlights.

Reserve Team Stalemate

FA Cup Provides Respite From League Action

Taken at The Dell, home of First Division Southampton, this photo shows Rovers in action against the home side in the fourth round of the FA Cup.

The match, even though it was against higher division opposition, provided a much-needed break from league action in one of the club's worst ever seasons.

At the time this game was played on 24th January 1981, Rovers had just one league success to their name, a 3-1 victory against Watford the previous November. Their interest in the League Cup had ended at the third round stage, though there had been a third round FA Cup win at Preston a few weeks before the trip to The Dell.

Although they lost 3-1 to Southampton, some 4,000 travelling fans saw Terry Cooper's side give a good account of themselves: *'Southampton opened the scoring in the 17th minute. Mick Channon crossed from the right, Steve Moran flicked the ball on and it was deflected past 18-year-old goalkeeper Phil Kite by Donny Gillies.*

'On 59 minutes, a superbly-flighted Charlie George chip from the right was chested down by Steve Williams and crashed past Kite.

'Twelve minutes later, Moran scrambled home Channon's right-wing cross and Southampton breathed a little more easily.

However, five minutes later, a sweetly taken goal by Geraint Williams from a right-wing cross by Gillies finally rewarded Rovers for their gallantry against probably the most feared side in the league at the moment.'

Saints boss Lawrie McMenemy was relieved to hear the final whistle: *'At 3-0, we shouldn't have let Rovers back in the game. But we did and, if they had scored again, the rest of the match would have been more nerve-wracking for us.'*

The attendance that day was 23,597 and Rovers lined up as follows: Kite, Gillies, Jones, Emmanuel, McCaffery, Hughes, Barrowclough, Mabbutt, Lee, Williams (G), Cooper. Substitute: Penny.

The Rovers players in the photo are goalkeeper Phil Kite, diving to smother a shot, watched by player-manager Terry Cooper, Mark Hughes (on the ground), Vaughan Jones and Donny Gillies watching events unfold in the foreground.

Southampton's Charlie George is beyond Kite, whilst another Southampton player can be seen through the mesh of the goal net.

As already mentioned, it was one of the club's worst seasons. In the aftermath of the Eastville fire in August 1980, Rovers won just five league games in the 1980/81 campaign and finished bottom of the Second Division.

A generation of supporters grew up watching Harold Jarman star on the right-wing for Bristol Rovers.

One of the most popular players to pull on a first-team shirt in the 1960s, his career took in 14 seasons and 452 league games. He also managed to score an incredible 127 goals, quite a record for a winger!

In fact, only Geoff Bradford and Alfie Biggs scored more goals that Harold, and only Bradford, Jack Pitt, Harry Bamford and Stuart Taylor appeared in more league games.

He was also a decent cricketer and played at county level, for Gloucestershire between 1961 and 1971.

There was a spell with Newport County after he left Eastville and then it was off to America where he turned out for New York Cosmos who, he likes to recall, replaced him with Pele when he left them!

He was associated with a number of clubs on his return to these shores and could add scouting duties for a number of top-flight clubs, including Manchester City and Blackburn Rovers, to his CV as well as forays into coaching and management on the local soccer scene.

He became caretaker manager of Rovers from December 1979 until April 1980 when, after he had saved the club from relegation to the Third Division, he was replaced by Terry Cooper.

He returned again between 1984 and 1986 as youth coach, but was made redundant as the club hit financial difficulties.

A true Rovers legend, this photo was taken in February or March 1980, during his spell as caretaker manager. The car sponsorship deal was described in the following way in the match programme at the time: *'Warners Motors, of Fishponds Road, Fishponds, presented manager Harold Jarman with a brand new Vauxhall Carlton Estate.*

'The sponsorship deal was negotiated by new financial director Graham Hole, who hopes that now Harold has steered Rovers out of the relegation zone, he will soon be steering the club towards the ultimate goal of Division One.'

He did indeed help Rovers avoid the drop as they finished the 1979/80 season with three clubs below them – Burnley, Charlton and Fulham were relegated to the Third Division. But the following year, under Cooper and after the Eastville fire, Rovers followed those three clubs through the relegation trap door.

Jarman's managerial record saw him win seven, draw nine and lose seven of the 23 league games he was in charge, and there was also one FA Cup tie, a third round defeat at the hands of Aston Villa.

Harold's Sponsored Car

A New Generation

I believe this photo was taken towards the end of the 1979/80 season as it features many of the young reserve and youth team players of the time.

Former Rovers player Bobby Jones stands on the left of the back row. He had returned to the club in February 1980, as youth coach. His good friend and former team-mate Harold Jarman was caretaker manager though he said at the time: *'Those are not the reasons I appointed him. He has a good knowledge of football and a tremendous enthusiasm for the game and for Bristol Rovers in particular.*

'Bobby has a good way with young players and has gained valuable experience of handling footballers during several years of management with non-league clubs.'

At the other end of the back row stands Dave Caines, appointed by Jarman at about the same time: *'Dave has taken over as physiotherapist. Like Bobby, he has a great enthusiasm for football and certainly knows his stuff on the medical side, having qualified through the FA treatment of injuries courses.'*

As for the players in the photo, here is the complete line-up:
Back (L-R): Bobby Jones, Dave Palmer, Jeff Shaw, Mark Hughes, Phil Kite, Mark Stevens, Mike England, Ashley Griffiths, Kevin Westaway, Dave Caines.
Front (L-R): Ian Holloway, Steve Williams, Geraint Williams, Micky Barrett, Tony Pulis, Gary Mabbutt, Martin Shaw, Gary Clarke, Steve Dean.

Only Jeff Shaw, Stevens and Dean never made a first-team appearance, whilst the combined total of first-team league appearances made by the rest of the players on view totalled 1,064 (includes substitute appearances) and one of them, Ian Holloway, later became manager of the club.

Palmer played only one first-team game against Wrexham in May 1979, but went on to enjoy a long career with Bath City. Mark Hughes is one of the select band of footballers to have played for both of Bristol's league clubs. Following his stint at Ashton Gate, he moved to Tranmere Rovers and played against Rovers in the 1990 Leyland Daf final at Wembley.

Kite, of course, has been the club's physiotherapist since 1996, Pulis has managed a number of clubs since his playing days and, at the time of writing, is in charge at Stoke.

Geraint Williams went on to manage Colchester United and Leyton Orient, while Mabbutt went on to gain England international honours and played at the very highest level for Tottenham Hotspur.

Tragically, Barrett died from cancer at the age of 24 and Westaway sustained serious head injuries in a road crash in Germany in the late 1980s.

Taken on Sunday 16th August 1980, this photo taken from the Tote End, shows how fire destroyed Eastville's South Stand.

The still-smouldering wreckage is quite visible and the roof looks as though it is about to collapse. The stand, of wooden construction, housed the offices and dressing rooms and nothing was saved.

In the aftermath of the fire, the whole structure was demolished and use of that side of the ground was restricted to an open terrace, making the once-proud sporting arena resemble a bomb site.

Five home games, including League Cup ties against York City and Portsmouth, were played at Ashton Gate before it was deemed that Eastville could once again host league football.

It was never the same as before though, with Portakabins for dressing rooms and a distinct lack of atmosphere at a venue that had held so many memories for generations of fans.

The season itself was a total disaster and Rovers finished bottom of the table, taking just 23 points from their 46 league games. There were few bright spots during a campaign in which only five league games were won, and a 4-3 third round FA Cup win at Preston was probably the highlight.

Writing in the 1981/82 Supporters Club Handbook, manager Terry Cooper was still able to find positives from a disastrous year: *'While not wanting to make excuses about last season, we never really recovered from the setback of the South Stand fire. Having painted it during the summer and stocked up with new kit, everything was geared to having a real go - and the day after our first match it was a charred skeleton.*

'The home dressing rooms are a very special place to footballers. We lost ours, found ourselves in Bristol City's for a while, then had to make do with Portakabins at Eastville for the rest of the campaign. Motivating the team in that confined space was not easy.

'But the season had its plus factors. The youngsters we brought in did well and will be a-year-older now in experience. In 18 months time we should have a capable squad of young lads, but unfortunately no one can buy time and we have a new season pressing on us.'

Ironically, Bristol City finished just seven points and one place above Rovers at the season's end and they too were relegated, so it definitely wasn't a good year for Bristol football.

It was to be another six years before the club left its dilapidated home and moved to play games at Bath's Twerton Park, but the writing was already on the wall – if there had been any walls left to write on!

The Eastville Fire

League Cup
Success At Ashton Gate

Following the fire which destroyed much of Eastville Stadium in August 1980, Rovers were indebted to neighbours Bristol City, who allowed them to play home games at Ashton Gate.

Of the five games played at there, the only victory came in a League Cup tie against York City on 3rd September 1980.

Trailing 2-1 from the first leg played at Bootham Crescent just a week earlier, Rovers knew that a single-goal victory would be enough to make further progress in the competition, provided that they didn't concede.

This photo shows Bob Lee, arms raised, celebrating the only goal of the second leg. He didn't score it, though, and that honour might have gone to Chic Bates, even though newspaper reports suggested that it could have been an own goal by visiting defender Steve Faulkner.

'York goalkeeper Eddie Blackburn almost denied Rovers a place in the third round of the League Cup.

'Because of his fantastic saves Rovers, who lost 2-1 in the first leg at York, were held to a 1-0 lead. That meant extra time and, with no further goals, eventual progress into today's third round draw by virtue of Aidan McCaffery's late goal at Bootham Crescent last week.

'The goal that put Rovers through came after 19 minutes. Stewart Barrowclough, later carried off with a gashed ankle that required 10 stitches, crossed perfectly from the right. Chic Bates rose high on the far post and, in textbook style, directed his header downwards. Steve Faulkner tried to clear off the line but only helped the ball into his own net.'

Bates, however, was adamant that he should be credited with the goal: *'I suffered enough frustration at the hands of the keeper, I'm claiming this one as the ball was over the line before Faulkner touched it.'*

Whilst he might have had a reasonable claim, the record books suggest that it was eventually credited to the York defender.

Watched by a crowd of 3,047, Rovers lined up follows: Thomas, Gillies, Bater, McCaffery, Mabbutt, Hughes, Barrowclough (Jones), Williams, Bates, Lee, Pulis.

Rovers were drawn against Portsmouth in the third round of the competition and after a goal-less draw at Ashton Gate, they were beaten 2-0 at Fratton Park.

Whilst it was to be a season to forget for Rovers, who were relegated to the Third Division at the end of the campaign, their visitors had an even worse time as they finished bottom of the Fourth Division.

I believe this photo was taken at the reserve team game against Chelsea, on 11th October 1980.

Chic Bates is the player in the foreground and Steve Harding is on the extreme right.

A late entrant to the world of professional football, Bates joined Shrewsbury in 1974 when he was 24-years-old. After almost four years at Gay Meadow, he moved to Swindon and it was from there that Rovers boss Harold Jarman brought him to Eastville in March 1980.

Writing in the matchday programme shortly after his arrival, Bates had this to say: *'I must admit that on my first visit to Eastville I wasn't impressed, but the more I see of the set-up here the higher I rate the club.*

'It was six weeks ago I came here with Swindon Town, for a reserve game. It was an evening kick-off, it was pouring with rain and I scored two as Swindon trounced Rovers 5-0.

'It was not the best of introductions to a club and when I was told, soon afterwards, that they wanted to sign me, I didn't have a very favourable impression of them.'

An ever-present for the final 11 games of the 1979/80 season, he scored twice and was in the starting line-up for the opening fixture of the following season and had made a further 18 appearances, adding another two goals, before he rejoined Shrewsbury in December 1980.

Once his playing career was over, he remained in the game as a coach and also worked as assistant to Lou Macari at a number of clubs, including Glasgow Celtic.

It was always his intention to go into the coaching side of the game, as he explained in that first Eastville interview: *'I am keen to help youngsters as I would like to remain in the game in a coaching capacity when my playing days are over. I took an FA preliminary course last summer and hope to gain a full coaching badge this year.'*

Bristol-born Steve Harding had played twice for Bristol City, twice more for Southend and eight times whilst on loan at Grimsby before joining Rovers in May 1977.

His Rovers career took in 38 league games and one goal, and he later spent time on loan at Brentford.

The game against Chelsea was just one of the 29 reserve-team appearances he made for the club in the 1980/81 season. Unfortunately, he and Bates were on the losing side that day, as the London side won 1-0.

Reserves Beaten By Chelsea

Channon Breezes In...
And Out!

The arrival of former England international Mike Channon on Sunday 17th October 1982 created quite a stir and this is how his signing was reported in Rovers matchday programme.

'Sunday mornings at our Hambrook training ground are normally very quiet – chief executive Gordon Bennett may be catching up on office work, Ray Kendall sorting his socks for the new week and physio John Higgs treating patients in his injury clinic, but otherwise there's usually very little activity.

'Not so on Sunday 17th October, the day Mike Channon joined Rovers in one of the most exciting signings struck in West Country soccer for many years.

'Press and radio reporters, photographers and TV cameramen, Rovers directors and most of the staff turned out to welcome the former Southampton and Manchester City striker – and manager Bobby Gould even had a dozen of the players in to provide the ex-England star with a full-scale training session.

'All this resulted from a sponsorship deal arranged by Bobby Gould with the St Catherine's Freezer Centre group, whose chairman, Tony Palmer, became a Rovers director earlier this year.

'It was in fact a continuation of an association between Mike and St Catherine's dating back to 1973, when Mike was the special celebrity who opened St Catherine's first store.'

Much was expected of the player who had nine England U-23 caps and 46 full caps to his name and it was hoped that his trademark 'windmill' goal celebrations would be a familiar sight at Eastville. After all, here was a striker who had scored 185 league goals for Southampton in two spells at The Dell, and another 24 in 72 games for Manchester City.

However, in just ten weeks with the club, he made only eight appearances. Four of those were from the bench – and there were to be no goal celebrations, home or away!

On 23rd December, Channon joined First Division Norwich on a free transfer. Manager Gould said: *'It would have been unfair of us to stand in the way of Mike having another fling in the First Division. We're very grateful for the tremendous contribution he made in helping revive Bristol Rovers in his time with us.'*

Channon commented as follows: *'There's some smashing people at Rovers. I wish the club every success.'*

In the photo shown here, Channon signs on the dotted line. Sat next to him is chairman Martin Flook, whilst behind him (L-R) are Graham Hole (director), Barry Bradshaw (vice-chairman), Bobby Gould (manager), Tony Palmer (director) and Alfred Hill (company secretary).

Once retired from the game, Channon pursued his other great sporting love, horse racing. He began working as an assistant trainer before becoming a licensed trainer in his own right and is based at West Ilsley stables near Newbury. In May 2012, he produced his first Classic winner when Samitar took the Irish 1,000 Guineas.

It's likely that this photo was taken at the club's Hambrook training ground in either 1981/82 or 1982/83.

The players featured are (L-R) Tim Parkin, Archie Stephens, Errington Kelly and, with his back to the camera, Brian Williams.

Parkin found his way to Eastville via Malmo and Almondsbury! He joined the Swedish club in January 1980 but in August the following year decided to move back to this country. However, there was a rule in place at the time which prevented Swedish-based players from moving to professional clubs outside of that country.

To get round this problem, Parkin joined non-league outfit Almondsbury Greenway and remained on their books for all of thirty minutes before signing for Rovers. He went on to make over 200 league appearances for the club before moving to Swindon in 1986.

Stephens was a popular figure at Eastville during his four-year stint with the club. Recruited from Melksham Town, he was 27 when he made his league debut against Chesterfield. He went on to score 40 goals in 127 league games and was transferred to Middlesbrough for a fee of £20,000 in 1985.

Kelly is the least successful member of the quartet, at least in terms of league games played. Another recruit from the non-league ranks, he joined Rovers in September 1981 and featured in five league games in the 1981/82 campaign. There were another 13 appearances the following season, when he scored three goals.

He joined Lincoln City in January 1983 and later played for Bristol City, Coventry City and Peterborough before moving to Sweden. His most successful time in this country came during his spell with Peterborough, where he scored 28 goals in 118 league games.

Williams also played for both Bristol clubs. He began his career with Bury, where he was an apprentice before signing his first pro contract. There were subsequent moves to QPR and Swindon before he arrived at Eastville in July 1981 and he played in 172 league games for the club, scoring 21 goals, before moving to Ashton Gate in the summer of 1985. After 77 league games in City's colours, his last port of call in league football was at Shrewsbury where he scored once in 65 league outings.

Training At Hambrook

Rovers' World Cup Winner

There aren't too many clubs at this level who can boast of having had a World Cup winner on their books.

However, in January 1983 manager Bobby Gould persuaded Alan Ball to join the club and the youngest member of England's World Cup-winning side of 1966 is pictured here trying on a Rovers club tie, at the insistence of Gould and watched by David Williams, Geraint Williams and Martin Thomas.

Ball was 37 when he arrived at Eastville and he made his debut against Chesterfield on 29th January 1983, scoring his first goal for the club against Plymouth Argyle the following month.

Writing in the matchday programme shortly after his arrival, he said: *'It might sound silly, but I got more excited the night before I made my Rovers debut than I had been for ages.*

'It made me realise how much I still enjoy football. It sounds corny, but I really do get a thrill out of playing. I don't understand why myself – it's a feeling I can't even scratch.'

He'd already had an unsuccessful spell as player-manager with Blackpool and made no secret of the fact that he wanted another chance as a manager. However, he promised to stay with Rovers until the end of the 1982/83 campaign. *'I've been linked with success most of my career, and I think the best way I can remind other clubs of that is by achieving a little bit more. If I can take a management job in the summer, leaving Bristol Rovers in the Second Division, I shall be a very happy man.'*

Ball had enjoyed a career in the top flight after starting his career with Blackpool. He later moved to Everton, Arsenal and Southampton and won a League Championship medal whilst at Goodison Park.

An England U-23 international, he won 72 full caps for his country and was rightly proud of his involvement in the 4-2 win over West Germany in 1966.

Rovers were his last league club and he made his final appearance in the last game of the season, a home fixture against Cardiff, which ended 1-1. Unfortunately he was unable to help the club gain promotion. Rovers finished in eighth position in the Third Division.

He went on to manage Portsmouth, Stoke, Exeter and Southampton and was later involved with BBC Radio Solent on Saturday afternoons, giving his views on the day's footballing events.

This is a rare photo of Les Bradd, scoring in his one and only league game for Rovers on 1st January 1983.

After scoring 125 goals in almost 400 league appearances for Notts County between 1967 and 1978, he had joined Stockport County and spent three years at Edgeley Park before a move to Wigan in May 1981.

Bobby Gould signed him on loan in the week leading up to the New Year's Day clash with Cardiff at Ninian Park, which ended in a 3-1 defeat for Rovers.

The newspaper report of the match stated that *'Bradd marked his debut with a goal and took up good forward positions.'*

With his new club trailing 2-0, Bradd hit the back of the net after 72 minutes. *'Rovers were awarded a penalty when Dwyer brought down Stephens but Dibble parried the spot kick taken by Brian Williams. The rebound fell to Bradd, who tucked home the loose ball.'*

Hemmerman scored twice for the home side that day, after 34 and 81 minutes. The third Cardiff goal was scored by Gary Bennett, three minutes before half-time.

The Rovers side for that Ninian Park, where there was a crowd of 10,968, was: Kite, Sherwood, McCaffery, Parkin, Williams (B), Holloway (Stephens, 62), Carter, Williams (G), Barrett, Bradd, Randall.

Troubled by a nagging hamstring after that game, Bradd never played for the club again. He said at the time: *'When I came to Rovers it was a good chance to join a side in the promotion race and prove that I've still got something to offer. I thoroughly enjoyed the game at Cardiff and thought we were*

unlucky to lose so heavily, but unfortunately I picked up an injury. It happened in the first ten minutes. I turned and felt a slight pull in my leg, and got a whack there late in the game, which aggravated it.'

This short letter from Bradd was published in Rovers' matchday programme for the game against Plymouth Argyle on 5th February 1983: *'I should like to publicly thank Bobby Gould for all the help I received during my month's loan with Bristol Rovers, and am very sorry the injury made a mess of things over the month.*

'I wish everybody at the club continued success, as you have a great crowd down there, and let's hope that it's promotion at the end of the season for you.'

Unfortunately promotion wasn't achieved and Rovers finished in eighth place in the old Third Division.

Bradd remains Notts County's all-time leading goalscorer and is still very much involved with the Magpies.

In 2012 he helped organize the club's 150th anniversary celebrations.

One Game, One Goal

On 5th February 1983, Rovers beat Plymouth Argyle 2-0 at Eastville.

The first goal was scored by Nicky Platnauer, the second by Alan Ball.

But it was the roles of non-playing substitute Archie Stephens and manager Bobby Gould that earned the three points – at least if you believe the match report!

'Archie Stephens made a significant contribution as Bristol Rovers took a step nearer promotion, yet he never left the substitutes bench.

'His exercises up and down the touchline, in front of the Eastville stand, prompted several players to raise their performances in the second half.

'Once Stephens peeled off his grey tracksuit and was noticed by his team-mates, Rovers clicked into top gear.

'On 66 minutes Micky Barrett burst down the right and passed inside to David Williams who eluded goalkeeper Geoff Crudgington, but when Gordon Nisbet cleared off the line, Nicky Platnauer calmly rammed in his fourth goal in three games.

'Stephens was then ordered by Gould to put his tracksuit on again.

'I was convinced the side scoring the first goal would win,' explained the manager afterwards. *'I used a bit of psychology. I had players wondering who was being substituted. None of them wanted to be pulled off and they all tried that little bit harder.'*

With two minutes of the game remaining, Ball scored Rovers' second goal of the afternoon. *'The entire stand rose to applaud the late goal that ended the Devon side's challenge. A swift run from Platnauer, a shot which Crudgington failed*

Psychology Earns A Win

to hold, and a deft tap-in from new favourite Alan Ball was an emotional climax.'

Platnauer, pictured above with Aiden McCaffery in the background, scored seven goals in 24 league appearances that season his first and last at Eastville. He had signed from Bedford Town, managed by Bobby Gould's brother Trevor, in the summer of 1982 and made his debut in the 2-1 home defeat by Lincoln City in September of that year.

When Gould moved on to manage Coventry City in the summer of 1983, he took Platnauer and Graham Withey with him.

He became something of a soccer nomad though, never staying at one club for any length of time. In all, his career saw him make league appearances for no fewer than 11 clubs. His 390 league appearances include 115 for Cardiff City and his final goals total reached 24, which included one against Liverpool in a 4-0 win over the Merseyside outfit.

The game at Eastville against Plymouth attracted a crowd of 6,556 and Rovers lined up as follows: Kite, Slatter, Parkin, McCaffery, Williams (B), Holloway, Williams (D), Ball, Barrett, Platnauer, Randall. Substitute (not used): Stephens.

One of many events to celebrate Rovers' centenary, in 1983 was a sponsorship appeal launched on the ss Great Britain in April of that year.

Pictured on board the famous old ship, and appropriately dressed in Pirate outfits, are Brian Williams, Archie Stephens, Phil Kite, Mike Barrett, Nicky Platnauer, Paul Randall and Keith Curle. I'm not sure, but I believe that Sean Penny is the player 'hiding' between Archie Stephens and Phil Kite.

Williams had played for Bury, QPR and Swindon before signing for Rovers in July 1981 and in his four years with the club, made 172 league appearances.

Stephens was 27 when Rovers signed him from Melksham Town, but he went on to become a big favourite with the fans and scored 40 goals in 127 league games whilst at Eastville. On leaving Rovers, he played for Middlesbrough, Carlisle and Darlington.

Phil Kite, of course, is now with the club as physiotherapist. Although he began his career with Rovers, he left in 1984 and his playing days took him to no fewer than another 12 clubs before his return, as physio, in 1996.

Barrett was a local player who joined the club in October 1979 and who went on to make 129 appearances for the club before he was, tragically, struck down by cancer and died in August 1984 at the age of 24.

Platnauer was with the club for just one season, 1982/83, when he made 24 appearances. His career is probably best described as nomadic, as he went on to play for another ten league clubs.

Randall was another popular player with the fans. Having been signed from Frome Town in 1977, he scored freely before a transfer to Stoke City in December 1978. He failed to settle in the Potteries and in January 1981 he returned to Eastville, after the club's supporters donated much of the money needed to bring him 'home.'

At the age of 28, he decided to retire from the pro game and enjoyed successful spells with Yeovil Town and Bath City before returning to his roots and playing Western League football.

At the time of writing, Curle is manager of Notts County. After making his Rovers debut against Chester in August 1981, he made a total of 32 league appearances for Rovers. It was only after he left Eastville that his career blossomed. He played for Torquay, Bristol City, Reading and Wimbledon before Manchester City paid the Dons a fee of £2.5m to take him to Maine Road and he won three full England caps whilst with them.

Aboard The ss Great Britain

Centenary Match

Formed in 1883, Rovers celebrated their centenary with a game against Tottenham Hotspur at Eastville on 18th April 1983 and the two squads are pictured here prior to kick-off.

Back (L-R): Ray Clemence, Garth Crooks, Simon Webster, Gary O'Reilly, Brian Williams, Jeff Sherwood, Micky Barrett, Neil Slatter, Tony Pulis, Graham Withey, Phil Kite, Glenn Hoddle, Alan Brazil.

Front (L-R): Chris Hughton, Ossie Ardiles, Gary Mabbutt, Steve Perryman, Aidan McCaffery, Archie Stephens, Paul Miller, Ian Holloway, Paul Randall, Tim Parkin, Tony Galvin, Ricky Villa, Graham Roberts.

The referee was Roger Milford, who is standing between his two linesman, Mr Coaten and Mr Wigginton, on the back row.

A special programme (priced 50p) was produced for the game and manager Bobby Gould recalled that the first transfer deal he negotiated as a manager was the one which took Gary Mabbutt from Rovers to Spurs.

In fact, the deal which had seen Mabbutt move to White Hart Lane for a fee reported to be £115,000 was the reason that Spurs were the club's opponents in the centenary match, for the game had been negotiated at the time of his transfer.

Kick-off was delayed to enable all of the 11,541 fans to get through the turnstiles and they witnessed a goal-less first half. Brian Williams gave Rovers the lead after the break, only for Garth Crooks to equalise for the visitors. After Paul Randall had once again given Rovers the lead, Bobby Gould decided to get in on the action and went on as a substitute. Spurs equalised through Steve Perryman just after his entrance, and Gary O'Reilly scored a last-minute winner, so it wasn't what you might call an inspired substitution!

As well as the football the fans, those who arrived early were able to watch a display by the Bristol Unicorns Youth Band and a free fall display by The Royal Green Jackets Parachute Team.

At half-time, a number of former Rovers players were introduced to the crowd, including Bill Dodgin, Frankie Prince, Stuart Taylor, Tom Stanton, Lindsay Parsons, Kenny Stephens, Trevor Jacobs, Andrew Evans, Peter Aitken, Ray Warren, Geoff Fox, Jackie Pitt, Peter Sampson, Ian Muir, Alfie Biggs, Ian Hamilton, Peter Hooper, Doug Hillard, Joe Davis, Ray Mabbutt, Bobby Jones, Ronnie Dix and Joe Walter.

Rovers were unable to clinch promotion in their centenary year and finished in seventh place in the old Third Division, seven points behind third-placed Huddersfield.

The club has, of course, celebrated its 125th anniversary since this game was played. That particular milestone was celebrated with a dinner dance, not a special match. So here's hoping for a game to mark the club's 150th birthday!

This photo shows a group of players training on the Eastville pitch under the guidance of Wayne Jones.

Apparently it was quite common for training sessions to take place on the pitch in those days, though it doesn't happen that often at any club now as they almost all train well away from their ground.

Jones, a former Rovers player whose career ended prematurely, has since worked as a physiotherapist at a number of clubs. He was assistant manager with Rovers, from June 1983 until 1985, and I believe this photo was taken during the 1983/84 season, possibly during pre season training in the summer of 1983.

On the left of the photo are David Williams and Mark Hughes.

Williams, whose Rovers career took in 352 league games, became player-manager of the club at the age of 28. He won Welsh schoolboy and youth international honours and also represented his country at U-21 and U-23 level before going on to win five full caps following his move to Norwich City in July 1985.

Hughes signed as an apprentice professional in 1978, though his stay at Rovers was punctuated by a loan spell at Torquay in 1984. He signed for Swansea before returning to Bristol, to play for City, in February 1985.

His stay at Ashton Gate was a brief one, however, and he moved on to Tranmere Rovers in September of that year.

Taking centre stage in the photo are Micky Barrett and Archie Stephens.

Barrett joined Rovers from local football in 1979 and quickly became a firm favourite with the Eastville crowd. By the summer of 1984 he has already appeared in 129 league games and seemed destined to play at a higher level.

However he was taken ill during pre-season training in the summer of 1984. Cancer was diagnosed and he died before the start of the 1984/85 campaign.

Stephens, 27 before he signed for Rovers, had spent his entire career on the non-league circuit prior to arriving at Eastville.

The final two players in the photo are Geraint Williams and Tim Parkin.

Williams arrived at Eastville in July 1978. A Welsh youth international, he also won two U-21 caps for his country. He appeared in 141 league games for Rovers before a move to Derby County in March 1985.

Parkin had played for Blackburn Rovers before joining FK Malmo and after making over 200 league appearances in a Rovers shirt, he went on to play for Swindon, Port Vale, Shrewsbury and Darlington.

Training On The Pitch

A Career Cut Short By Injury

Steve Bailey comes out on to the Eastville pitch for the last time, ahead of his Rovers team-mates and Coventry City, for his testimonial match on 15th November 1983.

The records show that Steve made just 16 league appearances for the club, and scored the only league goal of his career against Walsall in April 1983.

He made his first team debut in February 1982 while still an apprentice professional. Although he had signed a full-time contract by the time the club played Newport a month later, the registration forms hadn't arrived at league headquarters before kick-off and Rovers were deducted two points as a result.

All of his first-team games were played in the 1981/82 season, but when pre-season training began for the following campaign, the 18-year-old sustained a knee injury which eventually forced him to retire.

The right-sided midfielder had made a promising start to his professional career but, writing in his testimonial programme, he had this to say: *'The annoying thing is that I still don't know what went wrong with my knee. It kept swelling up for no reason, and then I remember a friendly game I went to cross the ball and it just locked. Since then there's been a succession of operations, but they have never found what's wrong or what's caused it.*

'There's no point in feeling bitter about it. I prefer to look at it that although I only played 16 league games, that's still more then most people ever have. It's down in black and white in the record books that I played in those games and scored a goal, and nobody can ever take that away from me.'

The Coventry side, managed by former Rovers boss Bobby Gould, also included former Rovers players Graham Withey and Nicky Platnauer, and the crowd of 1,859 saw Rovers take the lead courtesy of a Mike Barrett goal. However, the visitors equalised through Steve Hunt and Withey scored their winner in the second half.

Steve played the opening 45 minutes of the game and did well, according to newspaper reports: *'Bailey, whose knee will not stand up to the rigours of regular league football, gave an accomplished performance at right-back during the first half, when both teams fielded strong line-ups.'*

Gould went on as a substitute for Coventry with 25 minutes to go and the squads listed in the programme, apart from Bailey and Gould, were as follows:

Rovers: Kite, Bater, Williams, Pulis, Parkin, McCaffery, Holloway, Williams (G), White, Randall, Barrett, Stephens.

Coventry: Suckling, Roberts, Pearce, Grimes, Butterworth, Peake, Bennett, Gynn, Withey, Platnauer, Hunt.

Graham Withey and Nicky Platnauer, who had only left Eastville in the summer of 1983, made a quick return in November of that year.

Both had been signed for Coventry by former Rovers boss Bobby Gould, who had joined the Sky Blues on the final Saturday of the 1982/83 season.

The two are pictured here before the start of Steve Bailey's testimonial match, and it looks as though they might be getting a 'grilling' from fans who wanted to know why they had swapped Eastville for Highfield Road!

Welcoming them back for the game, Rovers skipper Aidan McCaffery had this to say: *'It is good to welcome our old team-mates Nicky Platnauer and Graham 'Sting' Withey back to Eastville, knowing they have both done well stepping up from the Third to the First Division.*

'When Nicky first arrived at the club from the Southern League, I had the feeling about him that he had the potential to play at any level of the game.

'And Graham is the type of player who will knock in goals against all types of opposition, although even he couldn't have believed he would reach the First Division quite so quickly after leaving non-league football.'

Withey had already scored goals in the First Division, against Spurs and West Bromwich Albion, and had this to say about his experience of playing at a higher level: *'I should probably have scored a few more, but basically I've just enjoyed playing in front of big crowds in the First Division.*

'I went to Coventry knowing that I was being bought principally as a reserve-team player, but with the promise that if I could keep scoring goals I could get a first-team chance. I didn't need to think twice about it. If I had not accepted this opportunity I think I might always have wondered whether I could have made it in the top flight or not.

'It's amazing how much every aspect of my game has improved since joining Coventry. I suppose working with better players and in a First Division set-up has made a big difference. I've started to feel like a First Division player. I've got a lot more confidence in myself, and it shows on the field.'

Graham and Nicky, who had both joined Rovers from non-league football, both left Highfield Road in December 1984.

Unlike their former colleague Steve Bailey, they both continued to play football for a number of years. As Rovers boss David Williams said at the time: *'Careers can be ended overnight. In some cases, as with Steve, they can be over almost before they begin.'*

Two Rovers Return

Centenary Celebration Match

Instead of an action shot from the match, I've selected this one of Newcastle's Kevin Keegan and Rovers' Brian Williams posing for the camera after the match between their respective sides at the end of a year of centenary celebrations.

Having already commemorated their centenary with a game against Spurs in April 2003, Rovers staged a celebration match against Newcastle on Tuesday 6th December 1983, a game which had been arranged as part of the deal that had taken goalkeeper Martin Thomas to St James' Park the previous March.

Thomas, made captain for the evening, led Newcastle out on to the pitch prior to kick-off, not anticipating that he was to be beaten five times by his old club. A Paul Randall hat-trick and a goal each from Ian Holloway and Mike Barrett secured a 5-4 win against the Magpies, for whom Peter Beardsley, John Trewick, Terry McDermott and David Mills were on target.

The crowd of 4,107 witnessed, according to former Rovers player 'Josser' Watling, an excellent game. *'My generation are always saying football today is not what it was when we were playing, but that was great entertainment and Rovers played really well,'* were his post-match comments.

Many former Rovers players were at the game, and the only two of the 1950s side missing were the late Harry Bamford and Vic Lambden, who had an abscess.

The Newcastle side boasted a number of talented players, including Beardsley and Keegan, and at the end of that season they finished in third place and won promotion to the First Division. Rovers, on the other hand, missed out on promotion to the Second Division, finishing in third place in Division Three.

It's also a day that Nicky Showering might well remember, as it was announced that he would not be offered a professional contract by Rovers. An 18-year-old midfielder, Showering had scored five goals in 16 reserve team appearances that season.

As for Thomas, although he played four games on loan at Middlesbrough in the autumn of 1984, he remained with Newcastle until October 1988 when he signed for Birmingham City. He also won a full Welsh cap to add to the youth and U-21 caps he had gained representing his country.

The squads on duty that evening were as follows:

Rovers: Cashley, Slatter, McCaffery, Parkin, Bater, Holloway, Williams (G), Williams (D), Barrett, Stephens, Randall, White, Williams (B), Hughes, Metcalfe.

Newcastle: Thomas, Carr, Haddock, Ryan, Carver, Anderson, Saunders, McDermott, McDonald, Trewick, Wharton, Beardsley, Ferris, Keegan, Mills, Waddle.

This photo shows Mark O'Connor in action against Bristol City at Eastville on 13th April 1985.

In the background, you can see that the Muller Road terracing has been reduced to make way for the Tesco supermarket development. One year later, Rovers were to play their last-ever game at the, by now dilapidated stadium.

Still, there were reasons to celebrate this match as Ian Holloway scored the only goal of the game to give Rovers all three points.

The match report said: *'Rovers can thank the initiative and vision of 18-year-old Paul Raynor for one of their most important wins over arch-rivals Bristol City.'*

Raynor, a deadline day loan signing from Nottingham Forest, explained that the goal which settled the match came after the players had watched City in action at Plymouth. *'We worked on Vaughan Jones taking the free kicks and our full-backs running through to beat the offside trap.*

'I found myself close to the ball after we'd been awarded a free kick and saw Mark O'Connor ready to get forward on his own down the left, so I swung it out to him and everything worked a treat, as Ian Holloway added the touch to Mark's cross for the winner.'

O'Connor refuted the suggestion that there was a suspicion of offside about the goal. *'City were taking chances by using that offside tactic in the windy conditions, and eventually we caught them out.*

'Their defenders were running forward, past me, and bringing our front men back with them when the ball was in the air.'

Apparently, the game was played in a gale-force wind. *'There was no chance of this being a football showpiece, but Rovers deserved their victory because every one of their players gave a workmanlike performance, whereas several City men failed to rise to the occasion.'*

Goalkeeper Ron Green revealed that City's half-time conviction that they had the game won contributed to their downfall. *'At half-time, we could hear the City players celebrating as though they had won the game. David Williams just told us to go out and play patiently and that we'd be OK, and that's just how it turned out.'*

The attendance for the game was 12,957 and they saw the following teams in action:

Rovers: Green, Slatter, Jones, Parkin, Bater, Holloway, Raynor, Williams (B), O'Connor, Randall, Bannon Substitute (not used): White.

City: Shaw, Stevens, Curle, Hughes, Newman, Pritchard, Stroud, Hutchinson, Walsh, Johnson, Riley (Neville).

O'Connor had been signed from QPR after a season-long loan at Exeter as a replacement for the late Micky Barrett. He quickly established himself as a regular in the first-team and in two seasons at Eastville, 1984/85 and 1985/86, he made 80 league appearances, scoring 10 goals.

A Derby Win

Last Eastville Derby

And now for a little bit of history - a photo taken just before the last-ever derby at Eastville on Tuesday 22nd April 1986.

The respective captains, Vaughan Jones of Rovers and City's Bobby Hutchinson, were probably wanting to get on with the game and to forget the formalities!

Jones and Hutchinson are pictured in the centre circle with the mascots and their parents, along with the match officials who, according to the programme, were Lester Shapter (referee) from Torquay and linesmen Mr J Byles (Oxford) and Mr J Roost (Bath).

The match, watched by 9,926 – Eastville's highest attendance of the season – ended 1-1 with Steve Neville putting City ahead and John Scales equalising for Rovers.

The teams lined up as follows.

Rovers: Green, Scales, England, Tanner (Noble), Parkin, Jones, Francis, Penrice, Morgan, White, Purnell.

City: Waugh, Llewellyn, Williams, Curle, Riley, Hutchinson, Neville, Walsh, Pritchard, Moyes, Harle.

Interestingly, there were quite a few connections between the clubs that evening. Rovers were managed by former City player Bobby Gould, whilst City boss Terry Cooper had previously managed Rovers.

Rovers' striker Trevor Morgan was a former City player, whilst City included two former Rovers players in their line-up, in Brian Williams and Keith Curle. Alan Walsh, a future Football in the Community Officer at Rovers, was also in the City side that evening.

Gerry Francis, later to become manager of the club and lead them to a Wembley final and promotion, was in the Rovers side, whilst the current Everton boss David Moyes played for City.

As for the captains, Vaughan Jones was to lead Rovers to those two triumphs mentioned above, in 1990, and ended his Rovers career with 12 goals and 381 league appearances to his name. A Welsh youth international, he also won two U-21 caps for his country.

Hutchinson appeared in 92 league games for City before leaving for Walsall in February 1987. Born in Glasgow, he had played for Hibernian before moving south of the border and, including his spell with City, he turned out for no fewer than eight English league clubs.

It's doubtful if many of the fans or players on duty that evening realised this would be Eastville's last-ever derby. Four days later, Rovers played Chesterfield in what turned out to be their final league game at what was by then a dilapidated old stadium and began a ten-year exile at Twerton Park, home of non-league outfit Bath City.

This photo was taken at Twerton Park on 17th September 1986, when Middlesbrough came to town and headed back home with all three points following their 2-1 win.

The Middlesbrough player in the foreground is former Rover favourite Archie Stephens, whilst the two Rovers players are John Scales and Trevor Morgan.

Geoff Twentyman played the fourth game of his fledgling Rovers career that day. *'Triallist Geoff Twentyman went into the game boosted by the offer of a two-year contract. The 27-year-old has earned the chance of a long term future at Bristol Rovers with three impressive performances.'*

'The offer is on the table and Geoff is considering it.' said manager Bobby Gould. *'He's done well on the field and is the type of character I want in the squad.'*

It wasn't the best of days for Gary Smart though. *'Part-timer Gary Smart's head was well and truly down after blowing his big chance to be Rovers hero.*

'Twice in the last ten minutes, following his arrival as substitute for veteran Kenny Hibbitt, the 22-year-old maintenance engineer had good chances to save the game for his team.

'First he volleyed the ball off target, then fired wide from close range after being sent clear by Trevor Morgan.'

Rovers went into the half-time break trailing after Bernie Slaven's 33rd-minute goal for the visitors. However, the equaliser, 'out of the blue' according to the match report, came on 62 minutes. *'Tarki Micallef, partnering Morgan up* front, scored his first goal for the club with a left-footed volley from Penrice's right-wing cross.'*

'Inevitably, though, former Eastville favourite Archie Stephens was to make his mark on his return to the West Country. He headed a Stuart Ripley centre from the right onto the far post and the rebound was headed in by Slaven for his second goal of the game.'

Speaking of his first goal for the club, Micallef had this to say: *'It was nice to score my first goal for Rovers, but it was a bit disappointing not to get at least a point after equalising against the odds.'*

Stephens had this to say: *'After playing at Bath quite a few times for Melksham and then Rovers, I never dreamt my next visit would be with Middlesbrough for a league match against Rovers. With the exception of myself we are a young side, and thoroughly deserved our win.'*

The Twerton Park crowd of 3,768 saw this Rovers side in action: Carter, Scales, Twentyman, Smalley, Jones, Alexander, Penrice, Hibbitt (Smart), Purnell, Morgan, Micallef.

Archie Returns

Play-off Hopefuls

There was a very good reason for taking this team photo at Bury's Gigg Lane on the final day of the 1988/89 campaign: it was to celebrate the fact that Rovers had already clinched a place in the end-of-season play-offs.

They travelled north on 13th May 1989 for their final league fixture with concerns that they hadn't scored in their last three games. And they made it four that afternoon as the game finished goal-less.

Gary Penrice sat the game out with an ankle injury, and, in this extract from the local press, you can see what they thought of the game. *'With Penrice missing, Rovers relied heavily on loan signing Dennis Bailey for finishing power. But the alertness which brought him nine goals in his first eleven games after arriving from Crystal Palace has been lacking in recent appearances.*

'Phil Purnell, returning after damaging knee ligaments, was not back to his best, but survived ninety minutes of league football without a setback which was important psychologically. And he has all this week to sharpen his fitness.'

It seems that the game was one of few chances and the only time Bury really threatened Rovers was in the 28th minute, when Liam Robinson's header from an inswinging corner beat Martyn, but Holloway cleared off the line.

Rovers, of course, went on to reach the play-off final that season. After a 1-0 home win against Fulham in the first leg of the semi-final, they trounced the London side 4-0 at Craven Cottage in the second leg.

Port Vale, though, were a different proposition in the final. They secured a 1-1 draw in the first leg of the final, at Twerton Park, and triumphed 1-0 at Vale Park to gain promotion.

Rovers, though, only had to wait another year before gaining promotion themselves as they ended the 1989/90 season as Third Division Champions.

As for the team photo which, strangely, wasn't used in either of the play-off programmes, Rovers lined up as follows:
Back (L-R) Ray Kendall (kit manager), David Mehew, Christian McClean, Nigel Martyn, Geoff Twentyman, Billy Clark, Devon White, Dennis Bailey, Roy Dolling (physio) Des Bulpin (assistant manager).
Front (L-R) Phil Purnell, Andy Reece, Vaughan Jones, Ian Holloway, Ian Alexander, Steve Yates.

For the game that afternoon, Clark and White were on the bench. White replaced McClean after 54 minutes, whilst Clark didn't get on.

This photo was taken at Vale Park, immediately after the play-off defeat against Port Vale on 3rd June 1989. The Rovers players acknowledging the fans are David Mehew, Nigel Martyn and Gary Penrice.

Rovers had finished in fifth place in the Third Division in the 1988/89 season, and qualified for the play-offs along with Port Vale, Fulham and Preston. There was no Wembley final in those days and the winners of the semi-finals played each other in a two-legged final.

Fulham were our opponents in the semi-final and a Gary Penrice goal gave Rovers a slender advantage after the first leg at Twerton Park. However, four days after that victory, Rovers travelled to Craven Cottage for the second leg and scored four second-half goals through Billy Clark, Ian Holloway, Dennis Bailey and Andy Reece to earn an emphatic victory and set up a final against Port Vale, who beat Preston 4-2 on aggregate.

Vale travelled to Twerton for the first leg and a crowd of 9,042 witnessed a 1-1 draw. Gary Penrice put Rovers ahead in the first half, but Vale equalised through Robbie Earle after the break.

The crucial second leg saw Earle score again in front of a crowd of 17,353 to give his side a 2-1 aggregate win and promotion to the Second Division.

Both teams fielded the same starting line-ups for both games, though McClean was used as a substitute, replacing Holloway in the first leg for Rovers, and Vale put Finney on in place of Porter in the second leg.

Rovers: Martyn, Alexander, Clark, Yates, White, Jones, Holloway, Mehew, Reece, Penrice, Purnell

Port Vale: Grew, Mills, Hughes, Walker, West, Glover, Jeffers, Earle, Futcher, Beckford, Porter, (Finney)

Rovers bounced back from the disappointment of that play-off defeat and went on to win the Third Division title the following season, though Martyn and Penrice had departed long before promotion was won. They both left the club in November 1989. Martyn moved to Crystal Palace, becoming the country's first £1m goalkeeper in the process. Palace reserve keeper Brian Parkin signed for Rovers as part of the deal and played a vital role in the Championship-winning side, while Penrice moved to Watford for £500,000.

Mehew remained at Twerton Park and was an important member of the promotion-winning side as he scored 18 league goals, many of which were matchwinners. Incredibly, he never scored more than once in any game.

Play-off
Heartache

A Goal Against His Former Club

He scored just six goals in 252 league appearances for Rovers, but the one against his former club Preston is probably regarded by Geoff Twentyman as the best.

Just moments after this photo was taken, Geoff's header was nestling in the back of the Preston net. David Mehew can't quite believe it and falls to his knees, whilst Devon White looks on in admiration!

The date was 16th September 1989 and it was the first of three goals scored by Rovers without reply that afternoon.

All three goals came in the opening 31 minutes. *'Preston had been under siege before Twentyman opened the scoring on 14 minutes.'*

'It was one of the sweetest moments of my career, to score against my old club for the first time,' said the central defender after the game.

'Gary Penrice got the second from eight yards, with the sharp finishing touch that is his hallmark, and Devon White powered in the third after his first shot had been blocked by the sprawling Andy Kelly.'

The win that afternoon saw Rovers go top of the league, having taken 12 points from their opening five games.

Making his Rovers debut that afternoon was Tony Sealy, who went on as a second-half substitute. A crowd of 4,350 at Twerton Park saw this Rovers team in action: Martyn,

Alexander, Yates, Twentyman, Jones, Mehew, Holloway, Reece (Sealy), Willmott, White, Penrice (Cawley).

Twentyman had joined Rovers, initially on trial, in the summer of 1986. His father, also Geoff, had played for Carlisle and Liverpool and went on to become chief scout at Anfield.

A brief spell as a schoolboy with Liverpool for Geoff Junior was followed by a non-league career which took in Formby and Chorley. It was while playing for Chorley that he was spotted by Preston.

He made a total of 98 league appearances whilst at Deepdale and his four goals, ironically, included one against Rovers in January 1985.

Signed on a free transfer by Rovers, he went on to become an integral member of the squad which clinched promotion at the end of the 1989/90 campaign. After being an ever-present in the side in 1988/89, he missed the play-off final that season when he attended his brother's wedding. But he was an ever-present again as Rovers clinched the Third Division title and made a Wembley appearance in the Leyland Daf final.

He left Rovers in 1993 and played, briefly, for Irish club Linfield before pursuing a career in broadcasting.

Ian Holloway persuaded him to return to the club as assistant manager in 1996, but at the end of that season Geoff resumed his broadcasting career.

Tony Sealy enjoyed a varied career in the game.
He started out at Southampton before joining Crystal Palace. A loan spell with Port Vale followed, then there was a permanent move to Queens Park Rangers, before another loan stint at Vale Park and two more loan spells with Fulham. He eventually joined the Cottagers in a permanent deal, moved to Leicester, was loaned to Bournemouth and also played for Sporting Lisbon and Braga before a move to Brentford.

He signed for Rovers in September 1989 and, on leaving in 1991, played football in Finland before moving back to Brentford.

Pictured here in action for Rovers against one of his former clubs, Brentford, Sealy picked up championship medals with four different clubs.

Rovers lost this game, played at Griffin Park on 20th January 1990, but went on to clinch the Third Division title and Sealy picked up his third championship medal at the end of the season.

He had already won a Second Division medal with Queens Park Rangers in 1982/83, and a Third Division medal with Bournemouth in 1986/87. He rejoined Brentford in October 1991 and helped them to the Third Division title at the end of the 1991/92 campaign.

Having featured in 19 league games in 1989/90, Sealy missed out on the club's first-ever trip to Wembley in the Leyland DAF Cup, having broken his leg in the game against Cardiff on 24th March.

At least he had the consolation of having already made a Wembley appearance, as he went on as a substitute for Southampton in the 1979 League Cup final, when the Saints lost 3-2 to Nottingham Forest.

That game at Brentford was one of only five losses in a remarkable season and, after the setback in London, Rovers were beaten just once more when they suffered a 3-1 defeat at the hands of Notts County on 26th April.

Here are just a few brief extracts from the match report. *'Rovers slipped to a third consecutive away defeat, which left them third in the table.*

'Christian McClean equalised for Rovers on 52 minutes, just two minutes after Simon Ratcliffe had scored for Brentford.

'Andy Reece got a touch to Paul Nixon's half-cleared cross. The ball fell to McClean, and he cracked in a first-time shot from close range.

'The winner came from Richard Cadette just five minutes from time.'

The side representing Rovers that day was: Parkin, Alexander, Twentyman, Yates, Jones, Mehew, Holloway, Reece, Nixon (Purnell), Sealy, McClean. Substitute: Cawley.

Only Championship Medals Will Do!

Home Debut for Carl

Having made his Rovers debut in the 1-0 win at Preston seven days earlier, Carl Saunders made his home debut for the club.

He made quite an impression as well! In front of a Twerton Park crowd of 6,223 on 18th February 1990, he scored both goals in a 2-0 win against Walsall. By all accounts, though, he could have scored six!

'Even before he opened the scoring, on 32 minutes, Saunders could have had a hat-trick. He shot wide of the target after just nine minutes, and again in the 29th minute, before being denied by a fine save by Fred Barber on 31 minutes.

'The breakthrough came from the resulting corner, when he got on the end of one of Devon White's near post flick-ons.

'Six minutes into the second half, Walsall's Stuart Rimmer struck a post but the ball was scrambled clear.

'Seven minutes from time, after he'd already gone close to scoring a second, Saunders struck again. White headed on a Jones free kick and he cracked it home.'

Rovers lined up as follows: Parkin, Alexander, Twentyman, Yates, Mehew (Byrne), Jones, Holloway, Reece, White, Saunders, Purnell.

Saunders had arrived at the club from Stoke City, for a fee of £70,000 and he was viewed as a replacement for Gary Penrice, who had signed for Watford in November 1989.

He had played on the wing and as a striker, but had also played at full-back and in midfield for Stoke.

He quickly became an integral member of the side, collecting a Third Division championship medal and appearing at Wembley in the Leyland DAF Cup just a few months after leaving the Potteries for the humble surroundings of Twerton Park.

He had an eventful game at Wembley, being denied a penalty and hitting the crossbar.

His Rovers career took in 142 league games and 42 goals, but he is probably best remembered for his FA Cup goals.

In a third round tie against Plymouth Argyle at Twerton Park on 5th January 1992, he scored four times as Rovers beat the Devon side 5-0. That win set up a clash with Liverpool in the fourth round and Saunders scored Rovers' goal in a 1-1 draw. The replay, at Anfield, saw him score a memorable 25-yard volley past Bruce Grobbelaar to give his side a half-time lead. However, Steve McManaman and Dean Saunders scored second-half goals for the Merseyside giants to progress through to round five.

After leaving Rovers he played, briefly, for Oxford and Walsall and also had a spell in Malta, where he turned out for Sliema Wanderers.

In this photo Ian Holloway takes what was, probably, the most important penalty in the club's history.

His successful spot kick put Rovers 3-0 up against local rivals Bristol City at Twerton Park and clinched promotion with just one game to play.

Victory at Blackpool four days later would confirm the club as Third Division champions. Anything less would have seen City clinch the title.

As we know, it all turned out just right as both Bristol clubs clinched final-day victories to gain promotion – Rovers as champions, City as runners-up.

The clash at Twerton Park, though, will forever be remembered by those who were there. The local press summed up the game in the following way:

'*The team that Gerry Francis created, largely from players discarded by other league clubs or rescued from part-time soccer, have brought Second Division football back to Bristol.*

'*And they did so in a style few could have predicted, thrashing neighbours City on a night no Rovers follower will forget.*

'*Two goals from Devon White, the striker built like a West Indian fast bowler, and just as lethal, plus a third penalty in four games by Ian Holloway settled the game inside little more than an hour.*'

White's first goal came on 25 minutes when Andy Llewellyn slipped and the striker scored from David Mehew's cross. His second was created by Carl Saunders, who beat Rob Newman and crossed for him to beat Ronnie Sinclair from ten yards.

Holloway's penalty came on 62 minutes, when Llewellyn handled Purnell's shot on the line, and he sent Sinclair the wrong way with his spot kick.

'*City destroyed by White lightning*' screamed the headlines the following morning, and the league table showed Rovers on top with 90 points, followed by City on 88. The Ashton Gate outfit beat Walsall four days later and would have won the title had Rovers not won at Bloomfield Road.

Even though Premiership sides Liverpool and Manchester City visited Twerton Park, and the likes of Wolves, West Ham and Blackburn Rovers came to the Roman City, 2nd May 1990 was, without doubt, the most dramatic evening of our ten-year stint at the non-league ground.

Watched by a crowd of 9,813, the teams that night lined up as follows:

Rovers: Parkin, Alexander, Twentyman, Yates, Jones, Mehew, Holloway, Reece, Purnell, White, Saunders. Substitutes (not used): Nixon, McClean.

City: Sinclair, Llewellyn, Newman, Humphries, Bailey (Honor, 62), Gavin, Rennie, Shelton, Smith, Morgan, Turner (Ferguson, 78).

Holloway has, of course, gone on to forge a career in management, firstly with Rovers followed by stints with Queens Park Rangers, Plymouth Argyle, and Leicester City. He created quite an impression in his only season in the Premiership as manager of Blackpool, where he remains in charge at the time of writing.

2nd May 1990

Blackpool Beaten

Most Rovers fans of a certain age will remember this goal, scored by Paul Nixon at Blackpool. Rovers had clinched promotion to the Second Division just a few days earlier, with a 3-0 win against Bristol City.

The win set up an intriguing final day of the season and on 5th May, Rovers travelled to Blackpool knowing that a win would clinch the Third Division title. More that 5,000 Rovers fans made the trip to Bloomfield Road, and as the official attendance was only 6,776, Blackpool could have been forgiven for thinking they were the away side!

David Mehew gave Rovers the lead after 28 minutes with his 21st goal of the season, and Phil Purnell made it 2-0 two minutes before half-time. The second half, described in one newspaper report as *one long party* remained goal-less until the final minute when Nixon, on as a substitute, scored a third with a sensational volley.

As you can see from the photo, Rovers supporters were already on the touchline waiting to mob the team at the end of the ninety minutes, and this is how the final act in an outstanding season was described in the local press. *'When Paul Nixon fired in the third goal in the 89th minute,*

Rovers fans couldn't contain themselves any longer. They poured on to the pitch hugging their heroes, each other and even the Blackpool players, who could only look on bemused. The Division Three title was theirs and they were loving every minute of it.'

The Rovers supporters saw this team – sporting blue and white quartered shirted – in action: Parkin, Alexander, Yates, Twentyman, Jones, Mehew, Holloway, Reece, Purnell (Nixon), White, Saunders. Substitute (not used): McClean

The goal was only one of six scored by Nixon in just over two years with the club. His only appearance in 1988/89 came against Northampton, when he was used as a substitute. In the promotion season, he appeared in 27 league games and there were another 16 appearances in 1990/91.

Prior to joining Rovers, Nixon who was born in the north east, had played as a part-time professional in New Zealand and won six full international caps for the Kiwis. On leaving the club he moved abroad again, and played football in Hong Kong.

Thirty seven years after topping Division Three (South) Rovers were crowned Division Three Champions in 1989/90 with a club-record 93 points.

Just a week after clinching the Third Division Title at Blackpool, and a week before their Leyland DAF final against Tranmere Rovers at Wembley, Rovers played a testimonial match for skipper Vaughan Jones against a team labelled as the Gerry Francis All Stars.

The match, at Twerton Park on Sunday 13th May 1990, attracted a crowd of 4,786 and they saw the All Stars win 2-1 thanks to goals by Paul Randall and Tommy Tynan, while Devon White replied for Rovers.

Randall was just one of four ex-Rovers players to 'guest' for the All Stars team, the others being Keith Curle, Gary Penrice and Tim Parkin.

Jones was presented with the Third Division trophy that afternoon, and skippered the side in the 2-1 defeat by Tranmere in the Leyland DAF final at Wembley the following Sunday.

The photo here shows the Rovers side who turned out that afternoon.

On the back row, sitting on top of the dugout are Christian McClean, Devon White, Andy Reece and Paul Nixon, whilst those standing are David Mehew, Carl Saunders, Ian Alexander, Ian Hazel, Ian Willmott, Marcus Browning, Gavin Kelly and Steve Yates.

In the front are Bob Bloomer, Vaughan Jones (with the Third Division Championship Trophy), Phil Purnell, Geoff Twentyman, Ian Holloway and Brian Parkin.

Four of these players – Holloway, Jones, Mehew and Twentyman – were ever-present in the title winning side, whilst Alexander missed just three games, Yates two and White six.

Saunders and Parkin were relative newcomers to the side. Parkin, signed as part of the deal which took Nigel Martyn to Crystal Palace, made 30 appearances. Saunders, who had arrived at Twerton Park in February, had featured in only 20 games. One week later, he was to win the Man of the Match accolade at Wembley, in spite of finishing on the losing side.

Of the others, most had played their part in a thrilling league campaign. Nixon, a New Zealand international, featured in 27 matches, Willmott 17, Purnell 22, and McClean 15.

Hazel made eight appearances, six of those coming from the bench, whilst the up-and-coming youngster Browning made just one substitute appearance.

Kelly had arrived, on loan from Hull in March and was a dependable understudy to Parkin, though had yet to feature in the first-team. He joined the club on a permanent basis in July of 1990.

Bloomer had also arrived in March and had yet to make his league debut, whilst Mehew was struggling with an injury when the testimonial match was played, but recovered in time to appear at Wembley.

The game against the All Stars came at the end of a testimonial year for Jones, and Rovers had played another game, earlier in the season, against Hambrook at Whiteshill Common.

Vaughan's Testimonial

Carried Off At Wembley

Rovers lost defender Ian Alexander in the opening 45 minutes of their first visit to Wembley in the Leyland DAF final in May 1990.

'Rovers hopes suffered a severe blow just before the break, when right-back Ian Alexander was forced out of the game with an ankle injury inflicted by Neil McNab's late challenge.

'With substitute Paul Nixon deployed in a wide midfield role, David Mehew switched to partner Ian Holloway in the centre with Andy Reece moving to the back four where he went on to do a good job.'

It was later revealed that Alexander had broken a bone in his ankle.

Born in Glasgow, Ian 'Jock' Alexander began his professional career with Rotherham, but moved back to Scotland to turn out for Motherwell in 1983. He also played for Morton before moving to Cyprus where he played for Pezoporikas Larnaca for one season.

He arrived at Twerton Park in the summer of 1986 as a right-winger. But once John Scales had been sold to Wimbledon, he became the club's first-choice right-back and went on to make 291 league appearances in his Rovers career.

A firm favourite with the fans, Alexander received three red cards in games against Bristol City, saved a penalty when he went in goal in place of the injured Brian Parkin, and

almost lost his life when he swallowed his tongue in an FA Cup tie against Fisher Athletic. A member of the 1990 championship-winning side, his day at Wembley against Tranmere came to a premature end, but he recovered and was fit for the club's first game back in the Second Division, against Leicester City, the following August.

While kit manager Ray Kendall carries what is probably the manager's suit, 'Jock' is helped off the pitch by physiotherapist Roy Dolling and Kenny Hibbitt, the man who wasn't going to be at the game!

Five days earlier Hibbitt, who joined the club as a player in 1986 and had been assistant manager to Gerry Francis for two years, was appointed manager of Walsall.

Hibbitt commented: *'Now I've left the club, it probably won't be right to stay involved. I don't want to disrupt anything. I had been looking forward to Wembley more than anything else and it's going to hurt now I've left.'*

He did attend though, and took his place on the bench next to Gerry Francis and it was clear, from his post-match comments that he enjoyed the experience. *'Getting to Wembley was a bonus. It would have been a sad day for me, whatever the result, but with these fans, Rovers must have a future. I played twice at Wembley, in League Cup finals, but have never seen anything like that sea of blue.'*

Adrian Boothroyd made just 16 appearances in a Rovers shirt after moving to Twerton Park from Huddersfield Town in June 1990 for a fee of £30,000.

The fee for the youngster was the highest Rovers had paid for a player since Terry Cooper had brought in Bob Lee and Aidan McCaffery, both of whom cost £70,000, some ten years earlier.

Boothroyd had graduated through the ranks at Huddersfield and had been offered a pro contract in July 1989. He made his debut for the Terriers in a 5-1 away win at Cardiff in March 1990 and went on to make a total of 10 league appearances for them prior to joining Rovers.

He suffered ankle injury problems in his early days at Twerton Park and it was March 1991 before he made his Rovers league debut in a 2-0 defeat at Oldham.

He joined Hearts in November 1992, but after just four substitute appearances for the Scottish outfit, he signed for Mansfield Town and made 102 league appearances whilst at Field Mill.

A move to Peterborough United followed his stint with the Stags but, at the age of 26, injury forced him to retire from playing.

It wasn't long before he began his coaching career and he went from coaching the U-17s to the same role with the U-19s, before becoming reserve-team coach with Peterborough.

His next move was to Carrow Road, where he became youth team coach with Norwich City. In November 2003, he took on the role of youth development officer and technical director with West Bromwich Albion, though his stay at The Hawthorns didn't last long, as he became first-team coach at Leeds United in the summer of 2004.

He graduated to his first managerial appointment with Watford in March 2005.

The photo here shows him in action in the 2-1 win over Oxford United, on 21st September 1991, at Twerton Park.

It was the only victory the club managed during the Martin Dobson's brief reign as manager.

However, Boothroyd appears to have played well in the match, as this extract from the report indicates. *'Most of the manager's gambles paid off. Billy Clark had a good game at the centre of defence, while Aidy Boothroyd proved a constant danger in his new role on the right flank. The decision to play Steve Yates, one of the game's most promising central defenders, in midfield, was brave but somewhat unsuccessful as the player struggled to find the authority he enjoys at the back.'*

Boothroyd was, briefly, the youngest manager in the Football League at the time of his appointment at Vicarage Road. However, it was a record he held for a short time as, nine games into the 2005/06 campaign, Bury gave 30-year-old Chris Casper control at Gigg Lane.

Since leaving Vicarage Road, he has managed Colchester and Coventry and, at the start of the 2012/13 season, was in charge at Northampton Town.

Boothroyd In Action

Cross Against Oxford

Pictured above is Steve Cross in action on his home debut for the club, against Oxford, on 21st September 1991.

The 1991/92 season had opened with two draws, but this was followed by five successive defeats, and this was the club's first win of the new campaign. The win lifted Rovers off the bottom of the table, above their visitors.

Victory came at a price though, as Vaughan Jones suffered a broken leg just eight seconds into the game.

Oxford took the lead after 35 minutes: *'Trevor Aylott, the 33-year-old striker on loan from Birmingham, flicked on Garry Smart's pass down the Rovers right-wing and Dave Penney had plenty of space and time to slip the ball past Brian Parkin.*

'Ian Alexander levelled three minutes later with a free kick, which was drilled low through the Oxford defensive wall, and past Kee's right hand.

'Steve Cross marked his home debut with a goal on 67 minutes, with a mis-hit lob from just outside the penalty area.'

'It wasn't the best of strikes, but if I'd hit it cleanly, it probably wouldn't have gone in.' said the midfield player before adding: *'I think the side is beginning to gel now. We played some very good football at times, although everyone knows the size of the task ahead.'*

Of the broken leg suffered by Jones, manager Dobson said: *'Vaughan was wearing the only shinpad approved by the Professional Footballers Association. It wasn't even marked, and obviously hadn't done the job it was supposed to.'*

Watched by a crowd of 4,854, Rovers lined up as follows: Parkin, Alexander, Twentyman, Clark, Jones (Archer), Boothroyd, Yates, Cross, Stewart, White (Browning), Saunders.

Steve Cross, who was born in Wolverhampton in December 1959, graduated through the ranks at Shrewsbury and made 262 league appearances during his time at Gay Meadow.

Derby County paid a fee of £75,000 to sign him in the summer of 1986, but his time with them was hampered by injury and in five years with the club, he made just 73 league appearances, 31 of which were from the bench.

Rovers also paid £75,000 to take him to Twerton Park, where he played in a total of 43 league games.

He joined the coaching staff during the ill-fated 1992/93 season, and was caretaker manager for three games in March 1993, between the departure of Malcolm Allison and the arrival of John Ward. He later became assistant manager to Ward but left the club, along with the manager, in the summer of 1996.

If you would like to order a copy of any of the images contained in this book,
please contact Keith Brookman whose contact details are listed below.
It would be helpful, when ordering, if you could quote the page number and
how many copies of the image you would like.
The cost per image depends on the size you would like and whether or not you would like it framed.
In addition there will be an additional charge to cover post and packing.
keithbrookman@btinternet.com
c/o The Memorial Stadium, Filton Avernue, Horfield, Bristol, BS7 OBF